South-Western
Writing for
Employment

Joyce Hing-McGowan, Director

Center for Business Teachers
San Francisco State University
San Francisco, California

Merle Wood

Education Consultant
Formerly of Oakland Public Schools
Lafayette, California

South-Western Publishing Co.

Developmental Editor: Mark Linton
Production Editor: Jean Findley
Associate Director/Design: Darren Wright
Production Artist: Sophia Renieris
Photo Editor/Stylist: Devore M. Nixon
Marketing Manager: Shelly Battenfield

Copyright (C) 1993
by SOUTH-WESTERN PUBLISHING CO.
Cincinnati, Ohio

ISBN: 0-538-70773-9

1 2 3 4 5 6 7 8 9 DH 98 97 96 95 94 93 92

Printed in the United States of America

 This book is printed on recycled, acid-free paper that meets Environmental
Protection Agency standards.

ACKNOWLEDGMENTS
Unit 1, page 103a, FPG International/Bernice Johnson; page 103b, BMPorter/Don Franklin
Unit 4, page 135, c Paul Buddle
Unit 6, page 161, c Bettman Archive
Unit 7, page 170, FPG International/Tracey T
Cover: Stamp design © 1991 United States Postal Service

Each of us requires the basic skills necessary to conduct our personal and business dealings. More and more adults are seeking to acquire these skills to improve both their personal interactions and employment opportunities. WRITING FOR EMPLOYMENT focuses on helping adults with this goal.

STRUCTURE AND ORGANIZATION ━━━━━━

WRITING FOR EMPLOYMENT presents clear objectives followed by short segments of material and exercises for immediate reinforcement. This competency-based approach enables students to achieve success frequently as they progress through the materials, building their self-esteem and competence.

This text-workbook prepares students to complete documents needed to apply for a job. They will prepare a personal profile, a resume, and learn to complete a job application. Students will also learn to complete forms and write memos and business letters—the most common written documents in the workplace.

The Pretest, Posttest, Glossary, Index, Answers, and Personal Progress Record facilitate and enhance independent student learning and achievement.

FEATURES OF *Writing For Employment* ━━━━━

WRITING FOR EMPLOYMENT is a complete and comprehensive package. It provides the student with learning material written to meet the unique needs of the adult learner, and the instructor with support materials to facilitate student success. The text-workbook includes the following features.

Appropriate Content. The realistic issues and skills emphasized throughout the text are paired with relevant examples and illustrations. A large typeface is used to make the material easy for the student to use.

Self-contained Approach. The text contains all the materials needed for self-paced and independent learning. The pretest and posttest allow students to evaluate their own skills. Answers for both tests and all exercises are in the back of the book.

Clear Objectives. Instructional objectives for each unit let students know what they will learn.

Exercises with Goals. Each unit contains short segments of instruction followed by exercises allowing students to immediately apply what they have learned. The end-of-unit activities provide applications for further reinforcement. All exercises include goals for students to measure their own skill development and success, providing student motivation and direction.

Study Breaks. Each unit also contains interesting study breaks which provide a refreshing break from study and yet contribute to the general literacy goal of the student.

Positive Summaries. Each unit ends with a summary of the student's accomplishments, providing encouragement and reinforcement.

Personal Progress Record. Students keep track of their own progress by recording their scores on a Personal Progress Record. Students can measure their success by recording their scores on evaluation charts provided for each unit. Whenever a student's total score for a unit is below the minimum requirement, the student may request a Bonus Exercise from the instructor for further study.

THE INSTRUCTOR'S MANUAL

The Instructor's Manual provides general instructional strategies and specific teaching suggestions for WRITING FOR EMPLOYMENT, along with supplementary bonus exercises and answers, testing materials, and a certificate of completion.

Bonus Exercises. Bonus exercises offer a second chance for all activities in the text-workbook. These bonus exercises enable instructors to provide additional applications to those students whose scores are below the minimum desirable for a unit. Answers to all bonus exercises follow, and all can be duplicated for student use.

Testing Materials. Two additional tests in the Instructor's Manual allow for more flexible instruction and evaluation.

Certificate of Completion. Upon completion of WRITING FOR EMPLOYMENT, a certificate of completion recognizes the student's success. This certificate has a listing of topics covered in the text. The manual contain a master certificate.

WRITING FOR EMPLOYMENT helps you invest in the future of your adult learners and meet your instructional needs.

CONTENTS

1994

Writing is an important method of communication. It is one of the ways you can express your thoughts and feelings. The look of a written document creates a first impression on the reader. The ability to communicate clearly in writing can make you more valuable to an employer. It is also an advantage to have this skill in your personal life.

HOW YOU WILL LEARN

WRITING FOR EMPLOYMENT will help prepare you to write the documents necessary to find a job. You will also learn to write some of the most common documents in the workplace.

Learn at Your Own Pace

You will progress through the lessons in WRITING FOR EMPLOYMENT while working at your own pace. Don't be concerned if you move faster or more slowly than other students. You are to work at *your* best pace and speed.

Learn Skills Successfully

The learning objectives before each lesson let you know what you are to accomplish. In each lesson you will study a new topic, and most include examples to help you. When you have shown that you understand the topic, move on to the next one. If you have not learned the material, you can do added study on that section. With this method, you can see how well you are doing as you move through each step in WRITING FOR EMPLOYMENT.

Complete Bonus Exercises

You may not reach your assigned goal on every practice activity. If this happens, review the lesson and then complete a Bonus Exercise. The bonus exercises cover the same material as the practice exercises in the book. They give you a second chance to reach your goal. Your instructor has copies of these bonus exercises.

Check Your Own Success

It is up to you to keep track of your success. After completing the activities in WRITING FOR EMPLOYMENT, you will check your work by looking up the answers in the back of the book. After checking your work, you will record your score on your Personal Progress Record which is also at the back of the book.

WHAT YOU WILL LEARN

As you progress through WRITING FOR EMPLOYMENT, you will study the type of writing needed in seeking a job and in common situations in the workplace. As your skills improve, you will see how writing can help you clarify your thinking, organize your thoughts, and explore how you feel. You might even discover that writing can be an exciting process.

PART ONE, Writing to Get a Job, includes four units on areas that will help you in your job search.

In *Unit 1, A Personal Profile*, you will write a detailed personal profile of your background and experience.

In *Unit 2, Resume*, you will develop a resume that is a summary of your background and qualifications.

In *Unit 3, Job Applications*, you will learn to complete the different parts of a job application.

Unit 4, Personal/Business Letters, presents the guidelines for writing a letter of application and an interview follow-up letter.

PART TWO, Writing on the Job, covers the most common written documents in the workplace.

In *Unit 5, Forms*, you will complete employment forms and business sales slips.

Unit 6, Memos, presents business memos and tips on how to be clear and concise in writing.

In *Unit 7, Business Letters*, you will learn guidelines for writing business letters.

PART THREE, Writing for Personal Development, gives you an opportunity to think about your personal goals.

In *Unit 8, Your Self-Improvement Action Plan*, you will develop short-term and long-term goals in twelve different areas of your life.

Good writing is a building process. WRITING FOR EMPLOYMENT will help you develop your skills so you will feel more self-confident about your writing ability.

SPECIAL FEATURES

WRITING FOR EMPLOYMENT has a number of special features. These features will help you learn and apply the material successfully.

Glossary

Key words and terms are in bold type throughout the text. You will also find them listed and defined in alphabetical order in a glossary in the back of the book.

Breaks from Instruction

Throughout WRITING FOR EMPLOYMENT, study breaks help you expand your understanding of the use of language. You can find them under the headings *Evolution of Writing* and *Getting Ready to Go to Work*.

Checkpoints and Activities

Exercises called *Checkpoints* help you check your understanding of a topic. You must meet the desired achievement goal before moving on to the next topic. At the end of each unit you will find activities called *Putting It Together*. These activities help you apply and reinforce the skills learned in the unit.

Margin Notes

The *margin notes* state a desired achievement goal for each Checkpoint and Activity. You should meet this goal before continuing with the rest of the unit.

Bonus Checkpoints and Bonus Activities

You may not reach the desired goal on every Checkpoint or Activity. If this happens, review the lesson again and then complete a Bonus Checkpoint or Bonus Activity. These Bonus features cover the same information presented in the unit and give you a second chance to succeed. Your instructor will supply the Bonus Checkpoints and Bonus Activities. Your instructor also has the answer key that you will use to check your work.

Answers

Answers to all the Checkpoints and Activities are in the back of WRITING FOR EMPLOYMENT. The color along the edges of the answer pages makes them easy to find. Use these pages to check your work. Always do the Checkpoints and Activities *before* you look at the answers. Use the answers as a tool to check your work—not as a means of completing the exercises.

Personal Progress Record

After checking your work, record your score on your Personal Progress Record. This form is also at the back of the book. After you complete a unit, you will be able to determine your level of success.

Certificate of Completion

When you finish WRITING FOR EMPLOYMENT, you may be eligible for a Certificate of Completion. Your instructor will explain the skill level required for you to earn this award.

READY TO START

You are now ready to start improving your grammar and writing skills. As you study these units, imagine how the skills you are learning can help you in a job or in your personal life. With study and practice, you will learn ways to use language to present your thoughts easily and directly. Your ability to write will always be a valuable and effective tool for you to use in communicating with others.

✔ CHECKING WHAT YOU KNOW

Take this pretest before starting WRITING FOR EMPLOYMENT. The 50 questions will tell you how much you already know about some of the writing you will do when looking for a job and when you are on the job. They will also tell you what you need to learn.

There is no time limit. When you finish, check your answers. Give yourself 1 point for each correct answer. Record your score on your Personal Progress Record. After completing the book, you will be able to see how much you learned.

Put a check mark by each item that would be included in a Personal Profile.

1. _____ Job Duties   9. _____ Height
2. _____ Social Security Number   10. _____ Special Skills
3. _____ Former Employers   11. _____ Organizations
4. _____ Schools Attended   12. _____ Certificates Earned
5. _____ Salary History   13. _____ Work History
6. _____ Names of Children   14. _____ Career Objective
7. _____ Telephone Number   15. _____ Hobbies
8. _____ Honors and Awards

Match the information in the left column with one of the parts of a Personal Profile and Resume in the right column. Put the correct letter in each space provided.

16. __c__ Ms. Julia Goldstein, Owner
Madison Grill
263 Madison
Sacramento, CA 95823-7139
(916) 555-8903

    a. Career Objective

    b. Educational Background

    c. Work History

17. __d__ Operate MBI Personal
Computer

    d. Skills and Abilities

18. __e__ Earned Certificate in
Word Processing

    e. Specialized Course and
Certificate

19. __a__ Want a position as an
Information Processor

20. _____   Bob's Restaurant
    375 16th Street
    Sacramento, CA 95818-6234
    (901) 555-7451
    1974–82

21. _____   Hobbies: Reading, guitar,
    and fishing.

22. _____   Columbia Community College,
    1987–89

f.   Interests, Talents, and
   Aptitudes

g.   References

Read the personal information on the following section of a job application. Put a check mark (✓) in the space provided next to the statements that are correct.

Last Name	First Name	Middle Name
Esparza		*Jane*

Address	Number	Street	City	State	Zip Code
3498 Sea Gull Drive			*Chicago, IL*	*60605-3498*	

Telephone Number(s)	Date of Application	Social Security Number		
555-4569	*10/25/92*	*348*	*76*	*2364*

_____ 23. Last and first names are included.
_____ 24. The state is included.
_____ 25. Area code is included with the telephone number.
_____ 26. A Social Security number is included.

Match the parts of personal/business letters in the left column with the definitions in the right column. Write the correct letter in the spaces provided.

27. _____ Salutation
28. _____ Complimentary close
29. _____ Reference initials
30. _____ Letter address
31. _____ Return address
32. _____ Keyed signature
33. _____ Body

a. Message of letter
b. Person sending letter
c. Writer's address
d. Initials of person who keyed letter
e. Name and address of person
   receiving letter
f. Greeting
g. Ending of letter

Read each of the statements. If it is true write a **T** in the space provided. If it is false write an **F** in the space provided.

_____ 34. One of the basic rules when completing forms is to read the form carefully before starting to write.

_____ 35. An Equal Opportunity Information Form includes information about disabilities.

_____ 36. Form W-4 is required by the Department of Labor.

_____ 37. Form W-4 tells your employer how much federal income tax should be withheld from your paycheck.

_____ 38. Form I-9, Employment Eligibility Verification, is required by the Immigration and Naturalization Service.

_____ 39. A sales slip shows what was purchased and how much was paid.

_____ 40. Memos are formal business letters.

_____ 41. A memo has a heading that includes these parts: TO, FROM, DATE, and SUBJECT.

_____ 42. A keyed signature is part of a business letter.

_____ 43. In a modified block style letter, the dateline begins at the left margin.

_____ 44. The ZIP code does not need to be included in the letter address.

_____ 45. The two-letter state abbreviation for Texas is TX.

_____ 46. You should proofread letters for spelling.

_____ 47. A goal is something you want to achieve.

_____ 48. In setting goals one of the questions to ask yourself is, "Where would I like to be?"

_____ 49. It is not necessary to develop long-term goals.

_____ 50. One of the categories to think about in developing goals is social relationships.

☞ *Check your work on page 98. Record your score on page 105.*

PART 1 **WRITING TO GET A JOB**

UNIT 1

A Personal Profile

MARKETING YOUR TALENTS

Marketing your talents is a six-step process for getting a job. The first step in marketing your talents is to look at what your qualifications are. You will need to write a detailed Personal Profile of your background. This profile will include your education and job experience. A Personal Profile will help you know what you have to offer an employer. The Personal Profile is for your own use. Do not send or give it to an employer. You will use it as a personal resource when you apply for a job.

The Personal Profile will give you an up-to-date written history of yourself. All the information about yourself will be organized and written in one place. As your experience changes, you will keep your Personal Profile updated.

The second step in marketing your talents is to prepare a resume. Resume preparation is presented in Unit 2.

The third step is to complete an application for a job. Job applications are presented in Unit 3.

The fourth step is to send a letter of application and resume to an employer. Letters of application are discussed in Unit 4.

The fifth step is the job interview. A job interview is your showcase for marketing your talents. During the interview, the employer judges your qualifications.

The sixth and last step is the job interview follow-up. Writing a follow-up letter is presented in Unit 4.

PARTS OF A PERSONAL PROFILE

Your Personal Profile will contain different types of information about yourself. In this unit, each section of the Personal Profile will be described. An example will be presented, and you will be asked to write this information about yourself. If you have access to a computer, you could key this information as it is presented.

Personal Information ━━━━━━━━━━

Personal information includes your name, current address, telephone number, Social Security number, date of birth, and driver's license number.

Example:

> Pat Sousa McClain
> 5235 Sky Ridge Avenue; Sacramento, CA 95818-4567
> (916) 555-4182 SS No. 536-58-6312
> Date of Birth—May 24, 1955 Driver's License No. B036 1533

CHECKPOINT 1-1

YOUR GOAL:
Get 5 or more points.

Write your personal information on a blank sheet of paper. Title this section *Personal Information*.

☞ *Check your work on page 98. Record your score on page 107.*

Educational Background ━━━━━━━

List the schools you attended—high school, trade or technical school, community college, or other special schools. Include the addresses and dates you attended.

Example:

> Luther Burbank High School
>   3500 Florin Road; Sacramento, CA 95823-3456 1969–1974
> Sacramento Vocational Center, Restaurant Program
>   9738 Lincoln Ave.; Sacramento, CA 95827-2313 1981–1982
> American College
>   4700 College Dr.; Sacramento, CA 95841-1234 1984–1986

GETTING READY TO GO TO WORK—Preparing for the Job Interview

- Learn about the company or business.
- Have a specific job or jobs in mind.
- Be on time—arrive a few minutes early.
- Prepare to answer questions about yourself and previous jobs.

CHECKPOINT 1-2

YOUR GOAL:
Get 3 or more points.

Write your educational background on a blank sheet of paper. Title this section *Educational Background.*

☞ *Check your work on page 98. Record your score on page 107.*

Specialized Courses and Certificates

What specialized courses did you take in school? When did you take them? List any certificates you received. Two specialized course classrooms are shown in Illustration 1-1.

Illustration 1-1

Specialized Courses

Example:

> Luther Burbank High School
>   Auto Mechanics (1971), Computer Applications (1972),
>   Electronics (1973), Accounting (1973–74)
>
> Sacramento Vocational Center, Restaurant Program
>   Certificate of Completion (1982)
>
> American College, Spanish I and II (1984–85)
>   Restaurant Management (1986)

CHECKPOINT 1-3

YOUR GOAL:
Get 3 or more
points.

Write any specialized courses you have taken on a blank sheet of paper. Also list any certificates you have received. Title this section *Specialized Courses and Certificates.*

☞ *Check your work on page 98. Record your score on page 107.*

Extracurricular Activities and Organizations

While in school, did you belong to any student organizations or groups? Did you play any sports, work on the school paper, or play in the band? Since you left school, have you been a member of any professional organization?

Example:

> Future Business Leaders of America (FBLA)—1973–1974
> FBLA Vice President—1974   Tennis Team—1972–1974
> California Restaurant Association—1984–Present

CHECKPOINT 1-4

YOUR GOAL:
Get 1 point for each item.

Write any extracurricular activities and organizations you were or are now involved in on a blank sheet of paper. Title this section *Extracurricular Activities and Organizations.*

☞ *Check your work on page 98. Record your score on page 107.*

Honors and Awards

What honors and awards have you received?

Example:

FBLA State Accounting Competition, First Place, 1974

Most Valuable Player Tennis Award, 1973

Spring Fair, Salad-Making Competition, Second Place, 1982

CHECKPOINT 1-5

YOUR GOAL:
Get 1 point for each item.

Write your honors and awards on a blank sheet of paper. Title this section *Honors and Awards.*

☞ *Check your work on page 98. Record your score on page 107.*

Work History

List all of your jobs including part-time, summer, and volunteer work. Give the name and address of each of your employers, job title or job duties, and supervisor. Include the dates you worked and the starting and final salary you earned. Give your reason for leaving the job. Your most recent or current job will be the last one on your list.

Example:

Sacramento Christian Church, 435 Watt Ave., Sacramento, CA 95823-1234;
    Child Care Volunteer—11/69–8/71
Job Title: Child Care Assistant
Supervisor: Mr. John Tinsley—(916) 555-2754

McDonald's, 3756 Arden Way, Sacramento, CA 95823-3254
Job Title: Fry Cook, Cashier—9/71–9/74
Supervisor: Mrs. Leah Gomez—(916) 555-5689
Starting Salary: $1.75 per hour Final: $2.00 per hour
Part-time job. Left for job at Bob's Restaurant

Bob's Restaurant, 375 16th Street, Sacramento, CA 95818-6234
Job Title: Restaurant Pastry Chef—10/74–2/82
Supervisor: Mr. George Clark—(916) 555-7451
Starting Salary: $5.00 per hour Final: $8.50 per hour
Left for job at Madison Grill

Madison Grill, 263 Madison, Sacramento, CA 95823-7139
Job Title: Assistant Kitchen Manager. Promoted to
Kitchen Manager in 1984. Supervise eight employees. 3/82–Present
Supervisor: Ms. Julia Goldstein—(916) 555-8903
Starting Salary: $21,000 Current Salary: $26,500

 CHECKPOINT 1-6

YOUR GOAL:
Get 1 point for each item.

Write all the information about your past employment on a blank sheet of paper. Title this section *Work History*.

☞ *Check your work on page 98. Record your score on page 107.*

Skills and Abilities

Do you have special skills? What do you do well? Do you operate any special type of equipment? Do you speak, read, or write another language other than English?

Example:

> Good at details; excellent organizational skills. Like working with people. Ten-Key Calculator and Macintosh Computer, Excel and Microsoft Word software. Speak, read, and write Spanish fluently.

✔ CHECKPOINT 1-7

YOUR GOAL:
Get 2 or more points.

Write your skills and abilities on a blank sheet of paper. Title this section *Skills and Abilities.*

☞ *Check your work on page 98. Record your score on page 107.*

Interests, Talents, and Aptitudes ▬▬▬▬▬

What are your special interests, talents, and aptitudes? What are your hobbies?

Example:

> Good with figures. Like math and accounting.
>
> Hobbies: Reading, fishing, playing tennis, and karate.

✔ CHECKPOINT 1-8

YOUR GOAL:
Get 2 or more points.

Write your talents, interests, and aptitudes on a blank sheet of paper. Title this section *Interests, Talents, and Aptitudes.*

☞ *Check your work on page 98. Record your score on page 107.*

Career Objective ▬▬▬▬▬

What kind of job do you want? List the types of jobs you feel best qualified for. What is your career goal? Possible job titles are shown in Illustration 1-2.

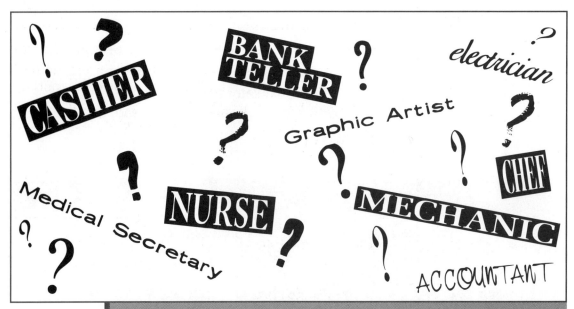

Illustration 1-2

Career Options—What Is Your Goal?

Example:

> Qualified for: Chef, Kitchen Manager
> Career Objective: Restaurant Manager

✔ CHECKPOINT 1-9

YOUR GOAL:
Get 2 or more points.

Write the jobs you are qualified for on a blank sheet of paper. Also write down your future career goal. Title this section *Career Objective*.

☞ *Check your work on page 98. Record your score on page 107.*

GETTING READY TO GO TO WORK—Personal Appearance for the Interview

- Be well groomed.
- Dress appropriately.
- Do not chew gum or smoke.

References

Most jobs require references. References are people who can say that you are a good worker. Ask permission before using a person's name as a reference. List former employers, instructors, or other people who can write a positive letter or answer questions about you. Do not use names of relatives. Include names, addresses, and telephone numbers.

Example:

Ms. Rita Chastain, Instructor
Restaurant Program, Sacramento Vocational Center
9738 Lincoln Ave.
Sacramento, CA 95827-2313
(916) 555-6648

Mr. George Clark, Kitchen Manager
Bob's Restaurant
375 16th Street
Sacramento, CA 95818-6234
(916) 555-7451

Ms. Julia Goldstein, Owner
Madison Grill
263 Madison
Sacramento, CA 95823-7139
(916) 555-8903

✔ CHECKPOINT 1-10

YOUR GOAL:
Get 3 or more points.

Write three references on a blank sheet of paper. Title this section *References*.

☞ *Check your work on page 99. Record your score on page 107.*

WHAT YOU HAVE LEARNED

As a result of completing this unit, you have learned that:

- A Personal Profile is a step toward marketing your talents.
- A Personal Profile includes—personal information; educational background; work history; skills and abilities; interests, talents, and aptitudes; career objective; and references.
- A completed Personal Profile is an up-to-date written history about yourself.

ACTIVITY 1-1   **YOUR GOAL:** Get 5 or more answers correct.

Match the information in the left column with one of the Personal Profile steps in the right column. Write the correct letter in each of the spaces provided. The first one is completed as an example.

- _c_ Mr. A. T. Herrera, Counselor
  Alhambra Technical School
  487 Oak Drive
  Columbus, OH 43210-5487
  (614) 555-9854

1. _____ Lang's Foreign Car Garage
   487 Sierra Avenue
   Bloomington, IN 47402-4891
   Job Title: Mechanic
   8/89–Present
   Supervisor: Ted Lang
   Salary: $11.50 per hour

2. _____ Speak and write Spanish

3. _____ Bank Teller Program,
   Received Certificate of
   Completion, 1989

4. _____ Licensed Practical Nurse

5. _____ Washington Adult School
   458 West Street
   Boise, ID 83720-4587
   1986–1987

6. _____ Photography, cooking,
   and oil painting

7. _____ Doris Chung, Vice President
   First Western Bank
   3486 Foothill Blvd.
   Houston, TX 77224-9532
   (713) 555-5211

a. Career Objective

b. Educational Background

c. References

d. Skills and Abilities

e. Specialized Courses and Certificates

f. Interests, Talents, and Aptitudes

g. Work History

☞ *Check your work on page 99. Record your score on page 107.*

UNIT 2

Resume

WHAT YOU WILL LEARN

When you finish this unit, you will be able to:

- Understand the purpose of a resume.
- Follow guidelines for preparing a resume.
- Develop a resume using a resume format and outline.
- Practice using resume language.

PURPOSE OF A RESUME

A **resume** is a summary of a person's background and qualifications. The purpose of a resume is to show an employer that a job applicant has the experience or education for the position. The resume lists the applicant's personal information, employment objective, education, work history, special skills, and references. A resume is sometimes called a *data sheet*.

Many jobs you apply for will require a resume. An effective resume "gets your foot in the door." It often leads to job interviews that you might not otherwise have.

CHECKPOINT 2-1

YOUR GOAL:
Get 4 or more answers correct.

Each of the following statements about the resume is either true or false. Write *True* in the space provided beside each true statement. Write *False* in the space provided beside each false statement. The first one is completed as an example.

__True__ • A resume is sometimes called a data sheet.

_____ 1. All jobs require a resume.

_____ 2. A resume includes work history and references.

14

_____   3. A resume is a summary of a job applicant's background and
                qualifications.

_____   4. A resume guarantees you an interview.

_____   5. Education is not listed on a resume.

☞ *Check your work on page 99. Record your score on page 107.*

GUIDELINES FOR WRITING A RESUME

A resume should summarize your qualifications and work history. The Personal Profile developed in Unit 1 will provide most of the information needed for writing your resume. The resume does not include everything that is on a Personal Profile. When you prepare your resume, follow these guidelines:

1. Keep your resume brief. Limit your resume to two pages.
2. Key your resume; never hand print.
3. Use a format that is readable and attractive in appearance. Leave white space on both sides, top, and bottom of the page.
4. Use good quality white paper.
5. Proofread carefully for correct spelling and punctuation.
6. Make neat corrections if you make any errors in keying.

RESUME FORMATS

There is no perfect resume format. The key is to present information that is brief, but complete. The resume should be attractive, neat, and easy to read. Two resume formats are used in this unit. Both formats use most of the information in the Personal Profile prepared in Unit 1. Look at the two different kinds of resumes shown in Illustration 2-1 and Illustration 2-2.

PAT SOUSA McCLAIN · ← ——— Name, Address, and
5235 Sky Ridge Avenue   Telephone Number
Sacramento, CA 95818-4567
(916) 555-4182

EMPLOYMENT OBJECTIVE: Restaurant Manager ← ——— Objective

EDUCATION:

1984 - 86 - American College; Sacramento, CA
             Spanish I and II, Restaurant Management

1981 - 82 - Sacramento Vocational Center   Education: List dates
             Restaurant Program   ← ——— attended. Complete
             Earned Certificate of Completion   address not needed.

1969 - 74 - Luther Burbank High School, Sacramento, CA
             Completed specialized courses in Auto Mechanics,
             Computer Applications, Electronics, and Accounting

EXPERIENCE:

1982 - Present - Madison Grill, Kitchen Manager
                Assistant Kitchen Manager, 1982–84
                Kitchen Manager, 1984–Present   Work Experience:
                Supervise eight employees.   List paid and unpaid
                                                      experience. List most
1974 - 82 - Bob's Restaurant, Pastry Chef   ← ——— recent first.
             Planned meals, developed menus, and worked with   Complete address
             food suppliers.   not needed.

1971 - 74 - McDonald's (Part-Time), Fry Cook and Cashier

SKILLS AND ABILITIES: Speak, read, and write Spanish ← ——— Special Skills,
                                                     Talents, and Abilities
REFERENCES:

Ms. Julia Goldstein, Owner   Mr. George Clark, Kitchen Manager
Madison Grill   Bob's Restaurant   References: List
263 Madison   375 16th Street   ← ——— three or write
Sacramento, CA 95823-7139   Sacramento, CA 95818-6234   *Available upon*
(916) 555-8903   (916) 555-7451   *request.* Complete
                                                      addresses and tele-
        Ms. Rita Chastain, Instructor   phone numbers.
        Restaurant Program, Sacramento Vocational Center
        9738 Lincoln Avenue
        Sacramento, CA 95827-6457
        (916) 555-6648

Illustration 2-1

Example Resume with Side Headings

LEE GUZMAN ROMERO

5987 Galisteo Dr.   Phone: (505) 555-4631
Santa Fe, NM 87504-3165   Evenings: After 5:30 p.m.

CAREER OBJECTIVE

Licensed Practical Nurse (LPN)

EDUCATION

Santa Fe Community College - Currently enrolled in Registered Nursing Program.   Have completed 24 semester units.

Voc-Tech Skills Center, Santa Fe. Completed Licensed Practical Nurse Program in 1990. Received State Certification, July 1990.

Engeneria High School, Guadalajara, Mexico, 1982 - 1986. Completed Nurse Assistant Program.

WORK HISTORY

Guadalajara Nursing Center   -   Certified Nurse Assistant
Guadalajara, Mexico   July 1986–August 1987

Delgado Convalescent Home   -   Certified Nurse Assistant
Santa Fe, New Mexico   November 1987 - June 1989

SPECIAL SKILLS

Spanish - Speak, read, and write.
Experience in home care, nursing homes, and hospitals.

REFERENCES

Available upon request.

Illustration 2-2

Example Resume with Centered Headings

GETTING READY TO GO TO WORK—Where to Find Out About Job Openings

- State Employment Offices
- Employers
- Civil Service Announcements
- Employment Agencies
- Newspaper Classified Ads

- School Placement Services
- Libraries
- Community Centers
- Labor Unions
- Friends and Relatives

RESUME OUTLINE

The example resumes in this unit show two commonly used formats. Each resume has similar basic information about the applicant. Study the following outline for developing your resume:

1. Personal Information
2. Career or Employment Objective
3. Education
4. Work History or Experience
5. Special Skills and Abilities
6. References

To complete the following Checkpoints, follow the format presented in Illustration 2-1 using side headings. Use the Personal Profile you developed in Unit 1 as a resource. Write the information on a blank sheet of paper.

CHECKPOINT 2-2

YOUR GOAL:
Get one point for each correct item.

Write your Personal Information. Put your name, address, and telephone number at the top of the page. Don't list weight, height, or date of birth.

☞ *Check your work on page 99. Record your score on page 107.*

CHECKPOINT 2-3

YOUR GOAL:
Get 1 point.

Write your Career Objective. Title this section *Career Objective* or *Objective*. If there is a specific job you are applying for, list this job.

☞ *Check your work on page 99. Record your score on page 107.*

CHECKPOINT 2-4

YOUR GOAL:
Get 10 points.

Write information about your educational background. Title this section *Education*. Include school names, addresses, dates of attendance, degrees, and certificates received.

☞ *Check your work on page 99. Record your score on page 107.*

CHECKPOINT 2-5

YOUR GOAL:
Get 10 points.

Write your work history—paid and volunteer work. Title this section *Work History* or *Experience*. Include the following for each job: job title, name and address of employer, and dates of employment. Begin with the most recent experience. Do not include salary information on a resume. This information goes on the job application—the next step.

☞ *Check your work on page 99. Record your score on page 107.*

CHECKPOINT 2-6

YOUR GOAL:
Get 1 point for each item.

Write your special skills and abilities. Include any special equipment and machines you can operate. Title this section *Special Skills*.

☞ *Check your work on page 99. Record your score on page 107.*

CHECKPOINT 2-7

YOUR GOAL:
Get 10 points.
References can be included on a resume. Another option is to note on your resume that your references are "available upon request." List the names, addresses, and telephone numbers of three references you could include. Title this section *References.*

☞ *Check your work on page 99. Record your score on page 107.*

RESUME LANGUAGE

Resume language is brief and to the point. A resume should be no longer than two pages.

To make your resume easy to read, use short, simple words. Complete sentences are not necessary. Resume writing is mastering the skill of saying a lot in a small amount of space. The following example is wordy:

> In 1990, after two years of experience as a salesclerk, I decided it was time to seek more responsibility. I applied for and received a promotion from salesclerk to sales manager in January.

Here is a brief version of the same paragraph:

Salesclerk 1988 - 90; Sales Manager 1990 - Present

In listing your skills, talents, and accomplishments, use words that describe. Words such as *organized, directed, supervised, operated,* and *designed* emphasize your job duties. Remember, you are trying to make an impression on the employer. You want to catch the employer's attention.

CHECKPOINT 2-8

YOUR GOAL:
Get 5 points.

Write the following information in resume language in the spaces provided:

1. Attended the Automotive Technical Institute in Detroit, Michigan, for two years. Completed the program and graduated in 1989. Received Automotive Mechanic Certificate.

   _____

   _____

   _____

2. Worked as an Auto Mechanic Assistant for one year. It was a full-time job at Yee's Foreign Car Repair from August 1986 to August 1987. The shop is located in Lansing, Michigan.

   _____

   _____

   _____

☞ *Check your work on page 99. Record your score on page 107.*

WHAT YOU HAVE LEARNED

As a result of completing this unit, you have learned to:

- A resume is needed for some jobs.
- Guidelines should be followed when preparing a resume.
- There is a standard resume format and outline.
- Resume language is brief and to the point.

ACTIVITY 2-1 YOUR GOAL: Get 5 or more answers correct.

The following sections are included in a resume: Education, References, Personal Information, Skills and Abilities, Objective, and Experience. Write the order in which they should appear in a resume in the spaces provided.

1. _____

2. _____

3. _____

4. _____

5. _____

6. _____

☞ *Check your work. Record your score.*

ACTIVITY 2-2 YOUR GOAL: Get 10 or more answers correct.

Underline the errors in the following resume information:

EDUCATION:

1. 1988 - 1990 - Tulsa County Area vocational School
   Tulsa, oklahoma
   Completed Building construction Prgram

REFERENCES:

2. Ms. Lydia Hill, Managr
   Hill's Building emporium
   3454 Main Stret
   Portland, or 97204-2101
   555-9479

3. mr. Gene osaki, Instructor
   Carpenter's apprenticeship Program
   458 Broadway, suite C
   eugene, OR 97405-6584
   (503) 555-396

☞ *Check your work on page 99. Record your score on page 107.*

22

UNIT 3

Job Applications

PURPOSE OF JOB APPLICATIONS

For most jobs, employers will ask you to fill out an application form. You will list the schools you have attended and any special training you have had. You will also list work experience and your references. Other information is also asked for on the form. Your completed job application tells about your qualifications. It helps an employer decide whether you should be given a job interview.

You will sometimes be asked to complete the job application at the place of business. In most cases, you can take the job application to complete at home.

How you complete the application shows the employer how well you can understand and follow instructions. It also shows the employer how neat you are. A sloppy application with errors may mean you cannot perform a simple job. Each business has its own job application form. Therefore, you need to read and follow instructions carefully.

The job application is usually the first thing an employer sees about you. You will want to make a good first impression. Study these tips on completing job applications.

1. Print the application in ink or key it. If you key the application, the keying should be slightly above the lines. Be as neat as possible.
2. Make sure your address is complete. The ZIP Code is part of your address.

23

3. Answer every question that applies to you. If a question does not apply, write *NA*, which means *not applicable*. NA tells the employer you did not skip answering the question.

4. Write the city and state where you were born under Place of Birth. Include the country if you were not born in the United States.

5. Take your Personal Profile with you. This information will be handy should you have to complete the job application at the business site.

6. Proofread your application. Be sure to spell correctly. The employer expects your application to show YOUR BEST WORK. Create a good impression.

7. Make a photocopy of your completed job application, if possible. You can use it as a quick guide when you have to complete other applications.

GETTING READY TO GO TO WORK—Verification of Your Right to Work

When you are hired for a job, you must furnish your Social Security card and one of the following documents within 72 hours of starting work:

- a card issued by federal, state, or local government showing your identity;
- U.S. military card or other draft card;
- driver's license or state-issued I.D. card with photo;
- school I.D. card with photo;
- U.S. passport;
- voter's registration card; or
- current Immigration and Naturalization Service (INS) forms with employment authorization stamp.

Unit 3   Job Applications

COMPLETING JOB APPLICATIONS

Job applications are usually two to four pages long. Most applications ask for the same information. The format of the job application will vary.

The following are examples of the most common questions asked on job applications. The Personal Profile in Unit 1 for Pat Sousa McClain was used in the following examples. Your Personal Profile will help you in completing the Checkpoint exercises in this unit.

Personal Information

The first section of a job application asks for your personal information. The information needed for this section includes name, address, telephone number, and Social Security number.

Example:

APPLICATION FOR EMPLOYMENT
(PLEASE PRINT PLAINLY)

The Civil Rights Act of 1964 prohibits discrimination in employment because of race, color, religion, or national origin. Public Law 90-202 prohibits discrimination because of age. The laws of some states prohibit some or all of the above mentioned types of discrimination.

Last Name McClain	First Name Pat	Middle Initial S.

Apt.	Number and Street 5235 Sky Ridge Avenue	City Sacramento

State CA	Zip Code 95818-4567	Can you, after employment, submit verification of your legal right to work in the United States? Yes

Are you over 18 years of age? ☒ Yes ☐ No	Telephone Number (include area code) (916) 555-4182	Social Security Number 536-58-6312

CHECKPOINT 3-1

YOUR GOAL: Get 4 or more answers correct.	Complete the application form with information about yourself. Read the instructions carefully. Use an ink pen.

APPLICATION FOR EMPLOYMENT
(PLEASE PRINT PLAINLY)

The Civil Rights Act of 1964 prohibits discrimination in employment because of race, color, religion, or national origin. Public Law 90-202 prohibits discrimination because of age. The laws of some states prohibit some or all of the above mentioned types of discrimination.

Last Name		First Name	Middle Initial
Apt.	Number and Street	City	
State	Zip Code	Can you, after employment, submit verification of your legal right to work in the United States?	
Are you over 18 years of age? ☐ Yes ☐ No		Telephone Number (include area code)	Social Security Number

☞ **Check your work on page 99. Record your score on page 108.**

Employment Desired ━━━━━━━

This section of a job application asks what job you are applying for. If you are interested in more than one job, list them. If there is a specific date you can begin work, write this in. It is appropriate to indicate an hourly wage, such as $7 an hour. An annual salary amount can also be written in. Be realistic on the salary you are asking for.

Many jobs are in the evening and on weekends. Many businesses are open seven days a week. Employers will want to know what you prefer and when you are available to work. Some jobs may be full-time or part-time. In the following example, *no restrictions* means that you can work anytime and any day of the week.

Example:

Position Applying For: **Restaurant Manager**	Date You Can Start **Immediately**	Salary Desired **$ 27,000**

Please check preferred schedule:
☐ I am available and desire to work FULL-TIME and do not have restrictions on my hours and days. (Complete Section B)
☐ I am available and desire PART-TIME work each week. (Complete Section A & B)

A   I am only available for PART-TIME because
☐ Student   ☐ Other Job   ☐ Other (explain) _____

B   Hours Available

	Monday	Tuesday	Wednesday	Thursday	Friday	Saturday	Sunday
"x" if no restrictions	✕	✕	✕	✕	✕		
I am available to work from	—— to ——	—— to ——	—— to——	—— to——	—— to ——	8a.m. to 5p.m	8a.m. to 5p.m.

✔ CHECKPOINT 3-2

YOUR GOAL:
Get 2 answers correct.

Complete the Employment Desired section of the application form. Think of a job to apply for or pick one of these positions:

- Auto Mechanic
- Legal Secretary
- Salesperson
- Electronics Assembler
- Teacher's Aide
- Dental Assistant
- Nurse
- Bus Driver
- Mail Carrier

Position Applying For:	Date You Can Start	Salary Desired

Please check preferred schedule:
☐ I am available and desire to work FULL-TIME and do not have restrictions on my hours and days. (Complete Section B)
☐ I am available and desire PART-TIME work each week. (Complete Section A & B)

A   I am only available for PART-TIME because
☐ Student   ☐ Other Job   ☐ Other (explain) _____

B   Hours Available

	Monday	Tuesday	Wednesday	Thursday	Friday	Saturday	Sunday
"x" if no restrictions							
I am available to work from	—— to ——	—— to ——	—— to ——	—— to ——	—— to ——	—— to ——	—— to ——

☞ *Check your work on page 100. Record your score on page 108.*

Education

The Education section of a job application asks about your schooling and training. Some applications will ask the highest grade you completed and the areas you studied. Some applications will ask for any special skills, such as speaking a foreign language, or any special equipment you can operate. If you have any certificates or any licenses, some applications ask for this information.

Example:

	Name	Graduate?
HIGH SCHOOL	*Luther Burbank High School*	☒ Yes
	Address	☐ No
	3500 Florin Rd., Sacramento, CA 95823-3456	
COLLEGE	Name	Graduate?
	American College	☐ Yes
	Address	☒ No
	4700 College Dr., Sacramento, CA 95841-1234	
OTHER	Name	Received Graduate?
	Sacramento Vocational Center	Certificate ☒ Yes
	Address	☐ No
	9738 Lincoln Ave., Sacramento, CA 95827-2313	

✔ CHECKPOINT 3-3

YOUR GOAL:
Get 2 answers correct.

Complete this section on Education with information about your schooling.

	Name	Graduate?
HIGH SCHOOL		☐ Yes
	Address	☐ No
COLLEGE	Name	Graduate?
		☐ Yes
	Address	☐ No
OTHER	Name	Graduate?
		☐ Yes
	Address	☐ No

☞ *Check your work on page 100. Record your score on page 108.*

Employment Record

The Employment Record section of a job application tells about your work history. If you have not had paid work experience, include volunteer work. Many applications will ask about previous salary earned, reason for leaving a job, and the duties of your different positions held. Most applications will ask you to begin with the most recent job experience.

Example:

Employment Record *All information including salary will be verified*		LIST PRESENT AND PREVIOUS POSITIONS AND VOLUNTEER WORK, STARTING WITH THE MOST RECENT POSITION.		
Present or last employer **Madison Grill**	Dates (mo./yr.) From **3/82** *To* **Present**	Current or last position **Kitchen Manager**	Salary (start/final) **$21,000–$26,500**	
Address **263 Madison; Sacramento, CA 95823-7139**			Telephone **(916) 555-8903**	
Duties **Responsible for operation of the kitchen. Develop daily menus and order supplies. Supervise eight kitchen employees**		Reason for leaving **—**		
Previous employer **Bob's Restaurant**	Dates (mo./yr.) From **10/74** *To* **2/82**	Current or last position **Restaurant Pastry Chef**	Salary (start/final) **$5–$8.50**	
Address **375 16th Street; Sacramento, CA 95818-6234**			Telephone **(916) 555-7451**	
Duties **Prepared desserts and bread items.**		Reason for leaving **Job at Madison Grill**		
Previous employer **McDonald's**	Dates (mo./yr.) From **9/71** *To* **9/74**	Current or last position **Part-Time Fry Cook**	Salary (start/final) **$1.75–$2**	
Address **3756 Arden Way; Sacramento, CA 95823-3254**			Telephone **(916) 555-5689**	
Duties **Grilled hamburgers, prepared sandwiches and salads.**		Reason for leaving **Full-Time job at Bob's Restaurant**		
Previous employer **Sacramento Christian Church**	Dates (mo./yr.) From **11/69** *To* **8/71**	Current or last position **Child Care Assistant**	Salary (start/final) **Volunteer**	
Address **435 Watt Avenue; Sacramento, CA 95823-1234**			Telephone **(916) 555-2754**	
Duties **Took care of small children while parents attended Sunday church service.**		Reason for leaving **Wanted a paying job.**		

CHECKPOINT 3-4

YOUR GOAL:
Get 7 or more
answers correct.

Complete the Employment Record of the job application with your work experience. If you have worked outside the United States, be sure to include this experience. Read the questions carefully.

Employment Record
All information including salary will be verified

LIST PRESENT AND PREVIOUS POSITIONS AND VOLUNTEER WORK, STARTING WITH THE MOST RECENT POSITION.

Present or last employer	Dates (mo./yr.) From	To	Current or last position	Salary (start/final)
Address				Telephone
Duties			Reason for leaving	

Previous employer	Dates (mo./yr.) From	To	Current or last position	Salary (start/final)
Address				Telephone
Duties			Reason for leaving	

Previous employer	Dates (mo./yr.) From	To	Current or last position	Salary (start/final)
Address				Telephone
Duties			Reason for leaving	

Previous employer	Dates (mo./yr.) From	To	Current or last position	Salary (start/final)
Address				Telephone
Duties			Reason for leaving	

☞ *Check your work on page 100. Record your score on page 108.*

References

Employers want to know about your character, work habits, and abilities. If you are a recent graduate, you can list instructors who know your schoolwork. Be sure you have the permission of the persons you use as references. You should include only those persons who can give you a good recommendation.

Example:

REFERENCES

Give names of two persons, not relatives or former employers who have known you for five years or more, that we may contact.

NAME	ADDRESS	TELEPHONE
Ms. Rita Chastain, Instructor Restaurant Program	9738 Lincoln Avenue Sacramento, CA 95827-2313	(916) 555-6648
Mr. George Clark, Kitchen Bob's Restaurant Manager	375 16th Street Sacramento, CA 95818-6234	(916) 555-7451
Ms. Julia Goldstein, Owner Madison Grill	263 Madison Sacramento, CA 95823-7139	(916) 555-8903

✔ CHECKPOINT 3-5

YOUR GOAL:
Get 3 answers correct.

Complete the References section of the job application.

REFERENCES

Give names of two persons, not relatives or former employers who have known you for five years or more, that we may contact.

NAME	ADDRESS	TELEPHONE

☞ *Check your work on page 100. Record your score on page 108.*

Signature

All applications require your signature. By signing the application, you are verifying that everything you have said is true. Should you falsify anything on the application, you could lose your job.

Example:

THIS APPLICATION IS NOT COMPLETE UNTIL THE FOLLOWING STATEMENT IS READ AND SIGNED.

I certify all the information furnished on this form is true. IF EMPLOYED, I understand that any falsification of this application may be cause for immediate dismissal.

Signed  _Pat Sousa McClain_ _____   Date __7/30/- -__

✔ CHECKPOINT 3-6

YOUR GOAL: Sign and date the Signature section of the application.
Get 2 answers
correct.

THIS APPLICATION IS NOT COMPLETE UNTIL THE FOLLOWING STATEMENT IS READ AND SIGNED.

I certify all the information furnished on this form is true. IF EMPLOYED, I understand that any falsification of this application may be cause for immediate dismissal.

Signed _____   Date _____

☞ *Check your work on page 100. Record your score on page 108.*

Other Information on Applications

You may be asked about any military service you have had. An employer will want to know if you have physical disabilities that may prevent you from performing certain types of jobs. Questions may be asked about any record of criminal convictions.

Many companies test all new employees for drug use. A list of prescription and over-the-counter medications may be requested.

GETTING READY TO GO TO WORK—Questions Asked During Interviews

- Why do you want to work for this company?
- What are your present job responsibilities?
- What do you do best?
- Why do you think you can handle this job?
- What are your future career plans?
- What are your hobbies and interests?
- What questions do you have about the job or our company?
- Why should you be hired for the job?

WHAT YOU HAVE LEARNED

As a result of completing this unit, you have learned:

- Why employers use job applications.
- The different types of questions asked on job applications.
- How to complete a job application.

ACTIVITY 3-1 YOUR GOAL: Get 8 or more answers correct.

1. Read the personal information on the following section of a job application. Put a check mark in the space provided next to the statements that are correct.

Last Name Romero	First Name Lee	Middle Initial G.
Apt.	Number and Street 5987 Galisteo Drive	City Santa Fe	

State CA	Zip Code 87504-6978	Can you, after employment, submit verification of your legal right to work in the United States?

Are you over 18 years of age? ☒ Yes ☐ No	Telephone Number (include area code) (505) 555-4631	Social Security Number

_____ a. Last and first names are included.

_____ b. The state is included.

_____ c. Area code is included with the telephone number.

_____ d. A Social Security number is included.

2. Read the following education information. Put a check mark in the space provided next to the statements that are correct.

HIGH SCHOOL	Name **Engeneria High Schol** Address	Graduate? ☒ Yes ☐ No
TRADE SCHOOL	Name **Vocational Technical Skils Center** Address	Graduate? ☒ Yes ☐ No

_____ a. Addresses are included.

_____ b. Information is written legibly.

_____ c. All words are spelled correctly.

_____ d. Yes or No boxes are marked.

3. Read the following employment information. Put a check mark in the space provided next to the statements that are correct.

Previous employer *Delgado* *Convalescent Home*	Dates (mo./yr.) From *11/87* To *6/90*	Current or last position *Certified Nurse Assistant*	Salary (start/final)
Address *428 Richards Drive; Santa Fe, NM 87504-4823*		Telephone *(505) 555-6133*	
Duties *Served meals, fed patients, made beds,* *bathed patients, completed patient charts.*		Reason for leaving *Job at St. John's Hospital*	

_____ a. Dates include month and year.

_____ b. Salary is included.

_____ c. Telephone number is included.

_____ d. Duties are included.

4. Read the following reference information. Put a check mark in the space provided next to the statements that are correct.

REFERENCES		
Give names of two persons, not relatives or former employers who have known you for five years or more, that we may contact.		
NAME	ADDRESS	TELEPHONE
Maria Donovan, Director of *Nursing; St. John's Hospital*	*428 St. Michaels Drive* *Santa Fe, NM 87504-6742*	
Dr. Alex Reyes *Delgado Convalescent Home*	*428 Richards Drive* *Santa Fe, NM 87504-4823*	

_____ a. Two references are given.

_____ b. Addresses include ZIP Codes.

_____ c. All words are spelled correctly.

_____ d. Telephone numbers are included.

☞ *Check your work on page 100. Record your score on page 108.*

UNIT 4

Personal/ Business Letters

WHAT YOU WILL LEARN

When you finish this unit, you will be able to:

- Write letters of application.
- Write interview follow-up letters.
- Address envelopes and fold letters.

LETTER OF APPLICATION

A letter of application is your introduction to an employer. It is a common way to ask for a job interview. Your letter will state what job you are applying for and why you are applying for it. You will write a letter of application

- when the employer you wish to contact lives in another city or town,
- as a cover letter when you are mailing a resume, or
- when you are answering a newspaper want ad or other job announcement.

Many people may apply for the same job, so your letter must create a good impression. It must attract attention, develop interest, and get action. Your letter will show how well you can communicate. Write all your letters so that they are interesting and accurate.

Guidelines for Writing Personal/Business Letters

In this unit, the block style letter format will be used. **Block style** is a format in which all letter parts begin at the left margin.

Letters can be written with two types of punctuation styles. **Mixed punctuation** requires a colon after the salutation and a comma after the complimentary close. The **salutation** is a greeting to the person receiving the letter. The

36

complimentary close is the ending in a letter. In **open punctuation,** no punctuation is used after the salutation or the complimentary close.

To write letters that create a good impression, follow these guidelines:

1. Key each letter neatly. Use correct grammar, spelling, and punctuation.
2. Include your address, the date, and your telephone number.
3. Address your letter to a specific person. Include name and title, company name, and address. If there is no name in a newspaper ad, you may call the business to get the name of the person you will write to.
4. Avoid starting the first sentence with the word *I.* Try not to overuse *I, me,* and *my* in your letter.
5. Limit your letter to one page.
6. In a letter of application, state the position you are applying for in the first paragraph. Close your letter by asking for an interview.
7. If you send a resume, use an enclosure notation.

Illustration 4-1 shows a person preparing to write a letter of application.

Illustration 4-1

Preparing to Write a Letter of Application

Parts of a Personal/Business Letter —————

There are five parts of a personal/business letter.

The return address and date are keyed about two inches from the top of the sheet. The **return address** is the writer's address and is keyed above the date.

The **letter address** includes the name and address of the person receiving the letter. The person's title and company name are included. Allow four to seven spaces between the date and letter address.

The **salutation** is a greeting to the person receiving the letter. Leave one blank space before and after the salutation.

The **body** is the message in a letter. Paragraphs are single spaced. Leave one blank space between paragraphs.

The **complimentary close** is the ending in a letter. Leave one blank space between the complimentary close and the last paragraph. Leave four blank spaces between the complimentary close and the writer's name. This space is for the writer's signature. The **signature** is the writer's name written in longhand. Be sure your signature is legible.

Illustration 4-2 shows the five parts of a business letter. Open punctuation is used in the letter.

CHECKPOINT 4-1

YOUR GOAL:
Get 5 or more answers correct.

Match the items in the left column with the definitions in the right column. Write the correct letter in each of the spaces provided. The first one is completed as as example.

____e____ ● Open punctuation	a. Greeting
_____ 1. Salutation	b. Writer's address
_____ 2. Body	c. Name and address of person receiving letter
_____ 3. Mixed punctuation	d. Ending of letter
_____ 4. Return address	e. No punctuation after salutation or close
_____ 5. Block style	f. Message of letter
_____ 6. Complimentary close	g. A colon after salutation and comma after close
_____ 7. Letter address	h. All letter parts begin at the left margin

☞ *Check your work on page 100. Record your score on page 108.*

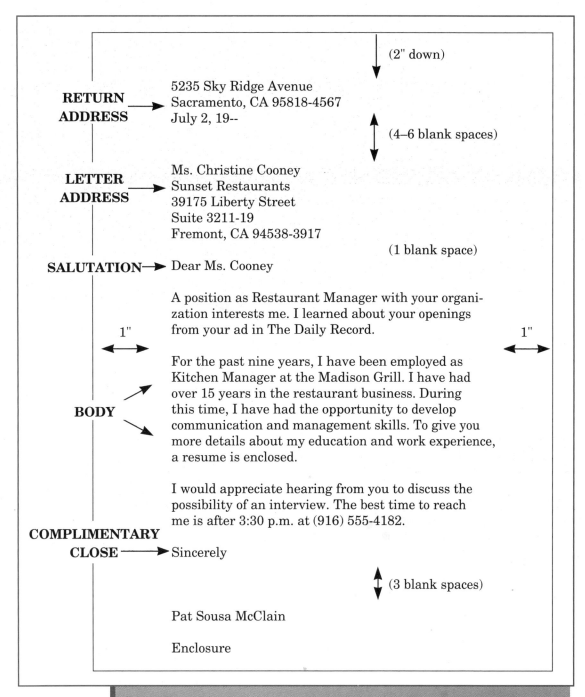

Personal/Business Letter with Open Punctuation

GETTING READY TO GO TO WORK—Tips for Women Going to Interviews

- Wear clothes appropriate for the job.
- Wear stockings or panty hose.
- Do not wear sandals or fancy shoes.
- Avoid excessive jewelry.
- Use make-up moderately.
- Do not wear overpowering perfume.
- Keep hair neat and away from your face.
- Have clean and shaped fingernails at a moderate length.

CHECKPOINT 4-2

YOUR GOAL:
Get 7 or more answers correct.

Read the following newspaper job ad. Write a letter of application for one of the jobs—supervisory trainee, cashier, or salesclerk. Write your letter on a blank sheet of paper. Use open punctuation. If you have access to a computer or typewriter, key your letter.

> **Supervisory Trainees, Cashiers, and Salesclerks**
>
> Office Products Emporium now has openings. Looking for energetic, responsible individuals who would like to grow with our team. Send resume or apply in person.
> Susan Ogata, Manager
> Office Products Emporium
> 4320 Newton Street
> Washington, DC 20010-2432

☞ *Check your work on page 100. Record your score on page 108.*

GETTING READY TO GO TO WORK—Tips for Men Going to Interviews

- Wear clothes appropriate for the job. If you wear a suit, wear a tie.
- Keep hair clean and neat.
- Trim beard and mustache.
- Do not wear overpowering cologne.
- Keep fingernails clean and trimmed.

INTERVIEW FOLLOW-UP LETTER

An interview follow-up letter should be sent to the employer after an interview. Your letter expresses your appreciation and thanks for the interview. A follow-up letter gives you one more chance to get the job. Sending a letter shows the employer that you have a sincere interest in the job.

Rules for Writing an Interview Follow-up Letter

Guidelines 1 through 5 for writing personal/business letters are used when writing an interview follow-up letter. In addition, your letter should include

1. a thank you for the interview, and
2. a statement to reaffirm your interest in the job and your availability.

Body of an Interview Follow-up Letter

The body of your follow-up letter will usually have three paragraphs.

The first paragraph will express your thanks for the interview. It will also state the position you applied for.

The second paragraph reaffirms your interest in the job. Say something about your education, work experience, and special skills.

The third and last paragraph will state your availability for the job. Illustration 4-3 is an example of an interview follow-up letter. The letter uses mixed punctuation.

✔ CHECKPOINT 4-3

YOUR GOAL:
Get 4 or more answers correct.

Each of the following statements about an interview follow-up letter is either true or false. Write *True* in the space provided next to each true statement. Write *False* in the space provided next to each false statement. The first one is completed as an example.

__True__ ● The follow-up letter has a salutation and complimentary close.

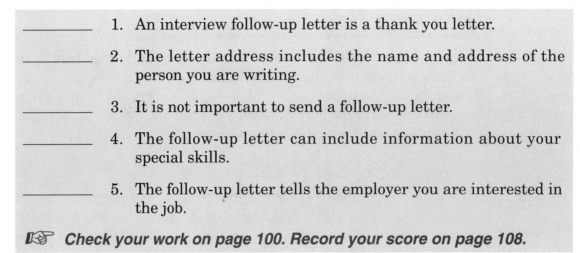

_____ 1. An interview follow-up letter is a thank you letter.

_____ 2. The letter address includes the name and address of the person you are writing.

_____ 3. It is not important to send a follow-up letter.

_____ 4. The follow-up letter can include information about your special skills.

_____ 5. The follow-up letter tells the employer you are interested in the job.

☞ *Check your work on page 100. Record your score on page 108.*

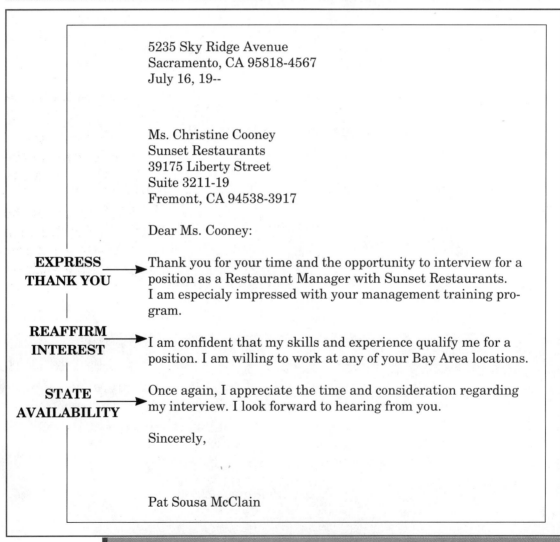

5235 Sky Ridge Avenue
Sacramento, CA 95818-4567
July 16, 19--

Ms. Christine Cooney
Sunset Restaurants
39175 Liberty Street
Suite 3211-19
Fremont, CA 94538-3917

Dear Ms. Cooney:

EXPRESS THANK YOU → Thank you for your time and the opportunity to interview for a position as a Restaurant Manager with Sunset Restaurants. I am especialy impressed with your management training program.

REAFFIRM INTEREST → I am confident that my skills and experience qualify me for a position. I am willing to work at any of your Bay Area locations.

STATE AVAILABILITY → Once again, I appreciate the time and consideration regarding my interview. I look forward to hearing from you.

Sincerely,

Pat Sousa McClain

Illustration 4-3

Interview Follow-up Letter with Mixed Punctuation

CHECKPOINT 4-4

YOUR GOAL:
Get 7 or more answers correct.

Write an interview follow-up letter. Your interview was last Tuesday with Ms. Susan Ogata, Manager. Write your letter on a blank sheet of paper. Use mixed punctuation. If you have access to a computer or typewriter, key your letter.

☞ *Check your work on page 101. Record your score on page 108.*

ADDRESSING ENVELOPES AND FOLDING LETTERS

After writing a letter, the next step is to prepare an envelope for the letter. The letter will then be folded and inserted into the envelope.

Addressing a Large Envelope

An envelope includes the return address of the writer. It also includes the name and address of the person who will receive the letter. Both addresses on the envelope should contain the two-letter state abbreviation and the ZIP Code. The state abbreviations will be covered in more detail in Unit 7.

The return address appears in the upper left corner of the envelope. The letter address begins on line 12 about 1/2 inch left of center. Both addresses are in all capital letters with no punctuation. Illustration 4-4 shows an example of the address format for a large envelope.

PAT SOUSA MCCLAIN
5235 SKY RIDGE AVENUE
SACRAMENTO CA 95818-4567

line 12 ↓   MS. CHRISTINE COONEY
1/2" left of center →   SUNSET RESTAURANTS
39175 LIBERTY STREET
SUITE 3211-19
FREMONT CA 94538-3917

Illustration 4-4

Addressing Large Envelopes

Folding a Personal/Business Letter

The correct procedure for folding a letter varies according to the size of the envelope. Illustration 4-5 shows the three steps for folding a letter into a large envelope.

Illustration 4-5

Folding Letters

Large Envelopes (Nos. 10, 9)

Step 1
With letter face up, fold slightly less than ⅓ of sheet up toward top.

Step 2
Fold down top of sheet to within ½ inch of bottom fold.

Step 3
Insert letter into envelope with last crease toward bottom of envelope.

CHECKPOINT 4-5

YOUR GOAL:
Get 3 or more answers correct.

Key an envelope for the letter you wrote to Ms. Susan Ogata in Checkpoint 4-4. Fold the letter.

 Check your work on page 101. Record your score on page 108.

WHAT YOU HAVE LEARNED

As a result of completing this unit, you have learned to:

● Specific guidelines should be followed when writing personal/business letters.
● There are five parts of a personal/business letter.
● After an interview, a follow-up letter should be sent.
● Addresses on envelopes are in capital letters.
● There is a correct way to fold a letter.

ACTIVITY 4-1   YOUR GOAL: Get 7 or more answers correct.

Pick a job from the Help Wanted section of your local newspaper for which you would like to apply. Write a letter of application on a blank sheet of paper. Use open punctuation.

☞ *Check your work on page 101. Record your score on page 108.*

ACTIVITY 4-2   YOUR GOAL: Get 3 or more answers correct.

Key an envelope for the letter you prepared in Activity 4-1. Fold and insert the letter.

☞ *Check your work on page 101. Record your score on page 108.*

PART

2

WRITING ON THE JOB

UNIT 5

Forms

EMPLOYMENT FORMS

In Unit 4, you learned about job application forms. There are three other forms to complete when you are hired for a job. One form asks for equal opportunity information. The other two forms are required by law: Form W-4, the Employee's Withholding Allowance Certificate, and Form I-9, the Employment Eligibility Verification.

Follow these basic rules when completing the forms:

1. Read the form carefully before starting to write.
2. Write neatly. Use a pen or key the information.
3. Be sure the information is accurate.
4. Sign your name legibly if your signature is required.

Equal Opportunity Information Form

All employers are required to provide an equal opportunity for employment to all persons. **Equal opportunity** means an employer will hire a person regardless of gender, sexual preference, race, creed, color, national origin, religion, handicap, or veteran's status. Employers keep track of this hiring practice. To do this, each applicant for a job is asked to complete a form. The form is completed on a voluntary basis. These forms vary with each company.

CHECKPOINT 5-1

YOUR GOAL:
Get 4 answers correct.

Review the completed Equal Opportunity Information Form on the left. Complete the blank form on the right with information about yourself.

Equal Opportunity Information Form

SEX	DISABILITY
[X] M	[ ] None
[ ] F	[ ] Sight impaired
	[X] Hearing impaired
ETHNICITY	[ ] Speech impaired
[ ] African American	[ ] Upper limbs impaired
[ ] Asian	[ ] Lower limbs impaired
[ ] Spanish Surname	[ ] Other (please specify)
[ ] White	
[ ] Pacific Islander	_____
[X] American Indian	**VETERAN**
[ ] Filipino	[X] No
[ ] Mexican American	[ ] Vietnam-era
[ ] Other (please specify)	[ ] Other Veteran
_____	[ ] Disabled Veteran

Equal Opportunity Information Form

SEX	DISABILITY
[ ] M	[ ] None
[ ] F	[ ] Sight impaired
	[ ] Hearing impaired
ETHNICITY	[ ] Speech impaired
[ ] African American	[ ] Upper limbs impaired
[ ] Asian	[ ] Lower limbs impaired
[ ] Spanish Surname	[ ] Other (please specify)
[ ] White	
[ ] Pacific Islander	_____
[ ] American Indian	**VETERAN**
[ ] Filipino	[ ] No
[ ] Mexican American	[ ] Vietnam-era
[ ] Other (please specify)	[ ] Other Veteran
_____	[ ] Disabled Veteran

☞ *Check your work on page 101. Record your score on page 108.*

Form W-4

Form W-4, Employee's Withholding Allowance Certificate, is a form completed for income tax withholding purposes. It is required by the Internal Revenue Service (IRS). Form W-4 tells your employer how much federal income tax should be withheld from your paycheck. Also on this form, you will declare your total number of allowances. An **allowance** is a person who is dependent on you for support. The more allowances you have, the less tax you will have withheld. Money withheld from your paycheck for federal income tax is paid directly to the Internal Revenue Service. State and city taxes may also be withheld from your paycheck.

A Personal Allowances Worksheet is part of Form W-4. It should be completed before filling in the W-4 section. You will give the employer only Form W-4—the certificate section.

You may claim yourself as an allowance. Other allowances can be claimed for your spouse or children. The following terms are included on the worksheet and Form W-4:

Dependents. People other than your wife or husband that you support. Children and elderly parents may be dependents.
Exempt Status. A claim that allows you to have no federal income tax withheld from your paycheck. You may claim to be exempt if you will not earn enough to owe any federal tax.
Head of Household. An unmarried person who pays more than 50 percent of household expenses.
Spouse. A wife or husband.

CHECKPOINT 5-2

YOUR GOAL:
Get 10 or more answers correct.

Review the completed Personal Allowances Worksheet and Form W-4, Employee's Withholding Allowance Certificate. Complete the blank form that follows with information about yourself.

A	Enter "1" for **yourself** if no one else can claim you as a dependent	**A** _____
B	Enter "1" if: { • You are single and have only one job; or • You are married, have only one job, and your spouse does not work; or • Your wages from a second job or your spouse's wages (or the total of both) are $1,000 or less. } . .	**B** _____
C	Enter "1" for your **spouse.** But, you may choose to enter -0- if you are married and have either a working spouse or more than one job (this may help you avoid having too little tax withheld)	**C** _____
D	Enter number of **dependents** (other than your spouse or yourself) whom you will claim on your tax return	**D** _____
E	Enter "1" if you will file as **head of household** on your tax return (see conditions under "Head of Household," above) .	**E** _____
F	Enter "1" if you have at least $1,500 of **child or dependent care expenses** for which you plan to claim a credit . .	**F** _____
G	Add lines A through F and enter total here. Note: *This amount may be different from the number of exemptions you claim on your return* ▶	**G** _____

For accuracy, do all worksheets that apply.
- If you plan to **itemize or claim adjustments to income** and want to reduce your withholding, see the Deductions and Adjustments Worksheet on page 2.
- If you are **single** and have **more than one job** and your combined earnings from all jobs exceed $29,000 OR if you are **married** and have a **working spouse or more than one job,** and the combined earnings from all jobs exceed $50,000, see the Two-Earner/Two-Job Worksheet on page 2 if you want to avoid having too little tax withheld.
- If **neither** of the above situations applies, **stop here** and enter the number from line G on line 5 of Form W-4 below.

----- **Cut here and give the certificate to your employer. Keep the top portion for your records.** -----

Form **W-4**	**Employee's Withholding Allowance Certificate**	OMB No. 1545-0010
Department of the Treasury Internal Revenue Service	▶ **For Privacy Act and Paperwork Reduction Act Notice, see reverse.**	19

1 Type or print your first name and middle initial	Last name	**2** Your social security number
Erlinda F.	*Peralta*	*258-53-8643*

Home address (number and street or rural route) *435 Cleary Street*	**3** ☐ Single ☐ Married ☒ Married, but withhold at higher Single rate. Note: *If married, but legally separated, or spouse is a nonresident alien, check the Single box.*
City or town, state, and ZIP code *Las Vegas, Nevada 89109-1435*	**4** If your last name differs from that on your social security card, check here and call 1-800-772-1213 for more information . ▶ ☐

5	Total number of allowances you are claiming (from line G above or from the Worksheets on back if they apply)	**5** *2*
6	Additional amount, if any, you want deducted from each paycheck	**6** $
7	I claim exemption from withholding and I certify that I meet **ALL** of the following conditions for exemption: • Last year I had a right to a refund of **ALL** Federal income tax withheld because I had **NO** tax liability; **AND** • This year I expect a refund of **ALL** Federal income tax withheld because I expect to have **NO** tax liability; **AND** • This year if my income exceeds $600 and includes nonwage income, another person cannot claim me as a dependent. If you meet all of the above conditions, enter the year effective and "EXEMPT" here . . ▶	**7** 19
8	Are you a full-time student? (Note: *Full-time students are not automatically exempt.*)	**8** ☐ Yes ☒ No

Under penalties of perjury, I certify that I am entitled to the number of withholding allowances claimed on this certificate or entitled to claim exempt status.

Employee's signature ▶ *Erlinda F. Peralta*   Date ▶ *September 1,*   , 19 --

9 Employer's name and address (Employer: Complete 9 and 11 only if sending to the IRS)	**10** Office code (optional)	**11** Employer identification number

A Enter "1" for **yourself** if no one else can claim you as a dependent . . . . **A** _____

B Enter "1" if:
- You are single and have only one job; or
- You are married, have only one job, and your spouse does not work; or . . **B** _____
- Your wages from a second job or your spouse's wages (or the total of both) are $1,000 or less.

C Enter "1" for your **spouse.** But, you may choose to enter -0- if you are married and have either a working spouse or more than one job (this may help you avoid having too little tax withheld) . . . . **C** _____

D Enter number of **dependents** (other than your spouse or yourself) whom you will claim on your tax return . . . . . **D** _____

E Enter "1" if you will file as **head of household** on your tax return (see conditions under "Head of Household," above) . **E** _____

F Enter "1" if you have at least $1,500 of **child or dependent care expenses** for which you plan to claim a credit . . **F** _____

G Add lines A through F and enter total here. **Note:** *This amount may be different from the number of exemptions you claim on your return* ► **G** _____

For accuracy, do all worksheets that apply.
- If you plan to **itemize or claim adjustments to income** and want to reduce your withholding, see the Deductions and Adjustments Worksheet on page 2.
- If you are **single** and have **more than one job** and your combined earnings from all jobs exceed $29,000 OR if you are **married** and have a **working spouse or more than one job,** and the combined earnings from all jobs exceed $50,000, see the Two-Earner/Two-Job Worksheet on page 2 if you want to avoid having too little tax withheld.
- If **neither** of the above situations applies, **stop here** and enter the number from line G on line 5 of Form W-4 below.

- - - - - - - - - - - - - - - - **Cut here and give the certificate to your employer. Keep the top portion for your records.** - - - - - - - - - - - - - - - -

Form **W-4**
Department of the Treasury
Internal Revenue Service

Employee's Withholding Allowance Certificate

► **For Privacy Act and Paperwork Reduction Act Notice, see reverse.**

OMB No. 1545-0010

19__

1 Type or print your first name and middle initial	Last name	**2** Your social security number

Home address (number and street or rural route)	**3** ☐ Single ☐ Married ☐ Married, but withhold at higher Single rate. **Note:** *If married, but legally separated, or spouse is a nonresident alien, check the Single box.*
City or town, state, and ZIP code	**4** If your last name differs from that on your social security card, check here and call 1-800-772-1213 for more information . ► ☐

5 Total number of allowances you are claiming (from line G above or from the Worksheets on back if they apply) **5** _____

6 Additional amount, if any, you want deducted from each paycheck . . . . **6** $ _____

7 I claim exemption from withholding and I certify that I meet **ALL** of the following conditions for exemption:
- Last year I had a right to a refund of **ALL** Federal income tax withheld because I had **NO** tax liability; **AND**
- This year I expect a refund of **ALL** Federal income tax withheld because I expect to have **NO** tax liability; **AND**
- This year if my income exceeds $600 and includes nonwage income, another person cannot claim me as a dependent.

If you meet all of the above conditions, enter the year effective and "EXEMPT" here . . ► **7** 19

8 Are you a full-time student? (**Note:** *Full-time students are not automatically exempt.*) . . . . **8** ☐ Yes ☐ No

Under penalties of perjury, I certify that I am entitled to the number of withholding allowances claimed on this certificate or entitled to claim exempt status.

Employee's signature ► _____ Date ► _____ , 19

9 Employer's name and address (Employer: Complete 9 and 11 only if sending to the IRS)	**10** Office code (optional)	**11** Employer identification number

☞ *Check your work on page 101. Record your score on page 108.*

EVOLUTION OF WRITING—Writing Instruments

In the very early days, people used chalky rocks to make marks and pictures on cliffs and on the walls of caves. As writing and drawing became more precise, the Egyptians invented "pens" made of bamboo reeds. The quill pen, made of goose feathers, replaced the reed pen. These pens could be found everywhere except in the Orient where the Chinese used brushes made from animal hairs. Around 1400 A.D., Europeans discovered that graphite could be used to mark on various materials. This discovery lead to the invention of the lead pencil.

Form I-9 —————

Any person hired for a job after November 6, 1986, must complete **Form I-9, Employment Eligibility Verification**. The Immigration and Naturalization Service requires this form. Form I-9 is a standard form used to verify that an individual is eligible to work in the United States.

The form asks for the employee's name, address, date of birth, birth name, and Social Security number. There is also a section that asks about the employee's immigration status. The term penalty of perjury appears on the form. Penalty of perjury means a person may be fined or go to prison for giving false information. The penalty of perjury also refers to your claim of being a citizen or alien who is authorized to work in the United States.

In addition to providing personal information on the I-9 Form, a person hired for a job is required to provide one or more documents that establish identity and employment eligibility. The documents an employer will need to examine are shown in Illustration 5-1.

One from List A

1. United States passport
2. Certificate of U.S. citizenship
3. Certificate of naturalization
4. Unexpired foreign passport with employment authorization

——————— OR ———————

One from List B	and	**One from List C**
1. State driver's license or I.D. with photograph 2. U.S. military identification card		1. Original Social Security card 2. Birth certificate 3. Unexpired INS Employment Authorization

Illustration 5-1

Documents Required for Employment Verification

CHECKPOINT 5-3

YOUR GOAL:
Get 8 or more
answers correct.

Review the completed Employment Eligibility Verification (Form I-9). Complete the blank form that follows with information about yourself.

EMPLOYMENT ELIGIBILITY VERIFICATION (Form I-9)

1 **EMPLOYEE INFORMATION AND VERIFICATION:** (To be completed and signed by employee.)

Name: (Print or Type) Last	First	Middle	Birth Name
Kimura,	Adam	S.	Kimura

Address: Street Name and Number	City	State	ZIP Code
324 Jackson	Austin	Texas	78731-1324

Date of Birth: (Month / Day / Year)	Social Security Number
March 22, 1953	651-37-9436

I attest, under penalty of perjury, that I am (check a box):

☒ 1. A citizen or national of the United States.
☐ 2. An alien lawfully admitted for permanent residence (Alien Number A _____).
☐ 3. An alien authorized by the Immigration and Naturalization Service to work in the United States (Alien Number A _____ .
or Admission Number _____ . Expiration of employment authorization, if any _____).

I attest, under penalty of perjury, the documents that I have presented as evidence of identity and employment eligibility are genuine and relate to me. I am aware that federal law provides for imprisonment and/or fine for any false statements or use of false documents in connection with this certificate.

Signature	Date (Day / Month / Year)
Adam S. Kimura	June 5, 19- -

EMPLOYMENT ELIGIBILITY VERIFICATION (Form I-9)

1 **EMPLOYEE INFORMATION AND VERIFICATION:** (To be completed and signed by employee.)

Name: (Print or Type) Last	First	Middle	Birth Name

Address: Street Name and Number	City	State	ZIP Code

Date of Birth: (Month / Day / Year)	Social Security Number

I attest, under penalty of perjury, that I am (check a box):

☐ 1. A citizen or national of the United States.
☐ 2. An alien lawfully admitted for permanent residence (Alien Number A _____).
☐ 3. An alien authorized by the Immigration and Naturalization Service to work in the United States (Alien Number A _____ .
or Admission Number _____ . Expiration of employment authorization, if any _____).

I attest, under penalty of perjury, the documents that I have presented as evidence of identity and employment eligibility are genuine and relate to me. I am aware that federal law provides for imprisonment and/or fine for any false statements or use of false documents in connection with this certificate.

Signature	Date (Day / Month / Year)

☞ *Check your work on page 102. Record your score on page 108.*

BUSINESS SALES SLIPS

One of the most common business forms is a sales slip. This form is a record for the customer and the business. A sales slip shows what was purchased and how much was paid. Some sales slips are designed for specific businesses. Others are general. They can be used for many types of businesses.

A sales slip designed for a beauty salon is shown in Illustration 5-2. The date, time, and customer name are written at the top of the form. All the services offered by the salon are listed. The services used by the customer are checked off. Because prices increase or change, the price must be written for each service. The hair stylist writes his or her name in the left column. Retail items such as shampoos, brushes, combs, and other products are written on the bottom.

Illustration 5-2

Sales Slip for
a Specific
Business

RIKI SALON

24 Sutter Lane
San Francisco, CA 94108-2102
(415) 555-4466

DATE _11/3_   TIME _1 p.m._
NAME _M. Carter_

STYLIST	SERVICE		PRICE	
Brandi	FEM HAIR CUT	✓	12	00
	MALE HAIR CUT			
	COLOUR			
	TINT			
	PERM			
	PART PERM WAVE			
	RELAXER			
	SHAMPOO/BLOW DRY			
	FACIAL			
	MANICURE/PEDICURE			
	MAKE-UP/LESSON			
	MISC			

RETAIL TICKET

STOCK	PRICE
Shampoo	2.50
TOTAL	

AMOUNT DUE		
SERVICE	12	00
RETAIL	2	50
TAX		18
TOTAL $	14	68

Services are not taxed. Sales tax is figured on the retail items only. Sales tax varies in each city and state. The total for services are added to the retail items plus tax. A final total is written last. Addition should be checked.

A general sales slip that could be used by many businesses is shown in Illustration 5-3. The date and customer's name and address are written at the top. The salesperson's name is written at the bottom. A cash or charge sale is checked. A charge sale usually means the customer is using a credit card to purchase the merchandise or service. If the purchase is to be mailed to another location, that information is included.

Illustration 5-3

General Use
Sales Slip

SPORTS UNLIMITED
458 PARK ST.
BOSTON, MA 02107-1234
(617) 555-3846

DATE 4/23   19

SOLD TO Pete Barnes
ADDRESS 42 Country Dr., Reno, NV 89501-3412
SHIP TO
ADDRESS

QUANTITY	DESCRIPTION	PRICE	AMOUNT
1	Nylon Jacket		39 99
1	Sunglasses		5 00
		TAX	2 70
		TOTAL	47 69

CASH ✓   CHARGE   SOLD BY Pam

Each purchase must be written in the space provided. Quantity, description, price of each item, and totals are written. Tax is calculated to find the amount of the total sale.

CHECKPOINT 5-4

YOUR GOAL: Get 10 answers correct.

Complete the sales slip. Include the following:

Date: Current date

Sold To: Barry Cowan

Address: 1248 Oak St.

Denver, CO

80232-1248

Sold By: KYT

How Purchased: Charge

Quantity: One pair

Description: J.V. Sports Shoes

Price: $29.95

Tax: $1.80

Total: $31.75

SPORTS UNLIMITED
458 PARK ST.
BOSTON, MA 02107-1234
(617) 555-3846

DATE		19
SOLD TO		
ADDRESS		
SHIP TO		
ADDRESS		

QUANTITY	DESCRIPTION	PRICE	AMOUNT
		TAX	
		TOTAL	

CASH	CHARGE	SOLD BY

☞ **Check your work on page 102. Record your score on page 108.**

WHAT YOU HAVE LEARNED

As a result of completing this unit, you have learned:

● What information is asked on an equal opportunity form.

● What Form W-4 is, and how to complete the form.

● How to complete an I-9 Employment Eligibility Verification form.

● How to complete two different types of sales slips.

ACTIVITY 5-1   **YOUR GOAL:** Get 4 or more answers correct.

Answer the following questions about the completed Form W-4 in the space provided.

Form **W-4**	**Employee's Withholding Allowance Certificate**	OMB No. 1545-0010
Department of the Treasury Internal Revenue Service	▶ For Privacy Act and Paperwork Reduction Act Notice, see reverse.	19

1 Type or print your first name and middle initial   **Last name**   **2** Your social security number

Leo   *Dameron*   **546-27-6831**

Home address (number and street or rural route)
1746 E. Date Avenue

3 ☒ Single ☐ Married ☐ Married, but withhold at higher Single rate.
Note: *If married, but legally separated, or spouse is a nonresident alien, check the Single box.*

City or town, state, and ZIP code
Tampa, Florida   *33624-1746*

4 If your last name differs from that on your social security card, check here and call 1-800-772-1213 for more information   . ▶ ☐

5 Total number of allowances you are claiming (from line G above or from the Worksheets on back if they apply)   **5**   *1*

6 Additional amount, if any, you want deducted from each paycheck . . . .   **6** $

7 I claim exemption from withholding and I certify that I meet **ALL** of the following conditions for exemption:
- Last year I had a right to a refund of **ALL** Federal income tax withheld because I had **NO** tax liability; **AND**
- This year I expect a refund of **ALL** Federal income tax withheld because I expect to have **NO** tax liability; **AND**
- This year if my income exceeds $600 and includes nonwage income, another person cannot claim me as a dependent.

If you meet all of the above conditions, enter the year effective and "EXEMPT" here . . . ▶ **7** | 19

8 Are you a full-time student? (**Note:** *Full-time students are not automatically exempt.*) . . . . **8** ☐ Yes ☐ No

Under penalties of perjury, I certify that I am entitled to the number of withholding allowances claimed on this certificate or entitled to claim exempt status.

Employee's signature ▶ *Leo Dameron*   Date ▶ *7/12*   , 19 – –

9 Employer's name and address (Employer: Complete 9 and 11 only if sending to the IRS) | **10** Office code (optional) | **11** Employer identification number

1. What is the employee's last name? _____

2. What is his Social Security number? _____

3. What is his marital status? _____

4. What city and state does he live in? _____

5. What is the total number of allowances he is claiming? _____

☞ *Check your work on page 102. Record your score on page 108.*

ACTIVITY 5-2   YOUR GOAL: Get 4 or more answers correct.

Answer the following questions about the completed sales in the space provided.

SPORTS UNLIMITED
458 PARK ST.
BOSTON, MA 02107-1234
(617) 555-3846

DATE **12/15**   19 – –

SOLD TO   *Rachel Acosta*

ADDRESS   *P.O. Box 523; Tucson, AZ 85713-0523*

SHIP TO

ADDRESS

QUANTITY	DESCRIPTION	PRICE	AMOUNT	
1	Shirt	15	15	00
2 pr.	Socks	4	8	00
1	Sports Cap	7	7	00
		TAX	1	80
		TOTAL	31	80

CASH ✓	CHARGE	SOLD BY *Bob*

1. What is the date of the sale? _____

2. What is the customer's name? _____

3. Was this a cash or charge sale? _____

4. How many items were purchased? _____

5. How much was the tax on the sale? _____

☞ *Check your work on page 102. Record your score on page 108.*

UNIT 6

Memos

BUSINESS MEMOS

A **memo** is a written communication used within an office or business. A memo is also called a *memorandum*. Memos are not as formal as letters. They may be written to communicate with just one person, or the same memo may be sent to several people. A memo may also be posted on a bulletin board for all employees to read.

Many businesses use standard memo stationery. Memos can also be on plain paper. Memos are keyed. A memo has a heading that includes these basic parts: TO, FROM, DATE, and SUBJECT. The *subject* line next to the subject head may or may not be capitalized. There are usually at least two blank lines between the heading and the first paragraph. A memo using company memo stationery is shown in Illustration 6-1.

The person sending the memo may initial the memo. The letters at the end of the memo are called *reference initials*. **Reference initials** tell who keyed the correspondence if it was not the sender. They are the first letters of the first and last names of that person.

COMPUTER
MARKETPLACE

Interoffice Memo

TO: All Employees

FROM: Arlene Lu, Personnel Director
         Ext. 4867

DATE: October 15, 19—

SUBJECT: HEALTH INSURANCE PROGRAM

A representative from the Stay-Well Health Plan will be here on November 10, 19—. The representative will talk about their new health plan. He will go over the cost of the rates for coverage.

The meeting is scheduled between 4:00–5:00 p.m., in Conference Room B. Please call me by November 8, if you will be attending. My number is Extension 4867.

jp

Illustration 6-1

Business Memo on Company Stationery

CLEAR AND CONCISE WRITING

Use clear and concise language when writing business letters and memos. Write as if you were talking to the person. Ask yourself, What do I want the reader to know, or what am I asking for? Use simple language. Do not use stiff or stuffy words. Use only the words needed to say what you mean. Short sentences are usually more effective than long, involved sentences. The following examples show how unneccessary words can be eliminated:

Say This	Do Not Say
enclosed	enclosed please find
thank you	want to thank you
please	we would appreciate
because	due to the fact that
we think	we wish to advise

CHECKPOINT 6-1

YOUR GOAL:
Get 4 or more answers correct.

Review the memo. Answer the following questions about the memo in the spaces provided.

M E M O

 Memorial Hospital and Medical Center

TO: All Employees

FROM: Arnold Stein, Manager
            Facilities Department

DATE: March 3, 19—

SUBJECT: Parking Lot C Resurfacing

Parking Lot C will be resurfaced on Friday, March 8. Please use Parking Lots A or B. Street parking is also available.

We regret this inconvenience and appreciate your cooperation during the resurfacing.

ef

---

1. Who is the memo from? _____

2. What is the subject of the memo? _____

3. What date is Parking Lot C being resurfaced? _____

4. Where should employees park? _____

5. What are the reference initials? _____

☞ *Check your work on page 103. Record your score on page 108.*

 ## CHECKPOINT 6-2

YOUR GOAL:
Get 4 or more answers correct.

Write a memo to your supervisor requesting two weeks' vacation. The two weeks are June 12–26. Your supervisor's name is Ms. Lilly Dong. Use the current date. If possible, key your memo. Use the memo stationery provided. Answer the following questions about your memo in the space provided.

Thompson PRODUCTS   PARTS · TOOLS · ACCESSORIES

Inter-Office Memorandum

TO:

FROM:

DATE:

SUBJECT:

1. Who is the memo written to? _____

2. What is the subject of the memo? _____

3. Did you key reference initials? _____

4. Who is the memo from? _____

5. Are the vacation dates included? _____

☞ *Check your work. Record your score.*

EVOLUTION OF WRITING—Early Typewriters

In 1868, Christopher Latham Sholes patented the typewriter. It only printed capital letters. Ten years later, the shift key was invented, and the typewriter could also print lowercase letters. In 1905, Sears sold a portable typewriter that was small enough to fit into a pocket. It cost $3.90.

NON-BIASED WRITING

In any type of business writing, titles and terms should be non-biased. Non-biased language does not favor female or male gender. Gender-neutral terms are used. The following are non-biased terms:

Say This	Do Not Say
work force	manpower
supervisor	foreman
firefighter	fireman
police officer	policeman
mail carrier	mailman
flight attendant	stewardess
humanity, everyone	mankind
sales representative, salesclerk, or salesperson	salesman

✔ CHECKPOINT 6-3

YOUR GOAL:
Get 9 or more answers correct.

Read each pair of terms in the following list. Write the best term to use in the space provided. The first one is completed as an example.

_____sales representative_____ • salesman/sales representative

_____ 1. mail carrier/mailman

_____ 2. fireman/firefighter

_____ 3. enclosed please find/enclosed

_____ 4. manpower/work force

_____ 5. want to thank you/thank you

_____ 6. we wish to advise/we think

_____ 7. due to the fact that/because

_____ 8. humanity/mankind

_____ 9. stewardess/flight attendant

_____ 10. supervisor/foreman

☞ *Check your work on page 103. Record your score on page 108.*

WHAT YOU HAVE LEARNED

As a result of completing this unit, you have learned:

- A memo is used within an office or business.
- Memos can be keyed on memo stationery or plain paper.
- Clear and concise language should be used.
- Non-biased language should be used.

ACTIVITY 6-1 YOUR GOAL: Get 4 or more answers correct.

Review the memo. Answer the following questions about the memo by writing *Yes* or *No* in the space provided. The first one is completed as an example.

TO: All Employees

FROM: Janet Russo, General Manager

SUBJECT: HOLIDAY PARTY

Plans for our annual Holiday Party are underway. This year's Holiday Party will be on December 16. It will be at the beautiful Palm Hotel.

Albert Montoya, Salesman in the Appliance Department, is organizing the event. Please call him if you can serve on one of the committees. We need six people to work with him. We want your ideas to make this event a big success and an enjoyable evening.

Please call Albert today!

___Yes___ ● Is the memo from Janet Russo, General Manager?

_____ 1. Does the heading include the date?

_____ 2. Should *Sales Representative* be used instead of *Salesman*?

_____ 3. Is a telephone number included for people to call?

_____ 4. Are reference initials included?

_____ 5. Are correct punctuation and capitalization used?

☞ *Check your work on page 103. Record your score on page 108.*

ACTIVITY 6-2 YOUR GOAL: Get 4 or more answers correct.

You are currently driving to work. There are several people from your company who live near you. You would like to start a car pool. You want to meet with anyone who is interested. Write a memo to your co-workers about your idea. Set a date, place, and time to meet. Use the memo stationery provided. Answer the questions about your memo that follow in the space provided.

Memo

*C*arla's
Cabinet
onstruction

TO:

FROM:

DATE:

SUBJECT:

---

1. Who is the memo written to? _____

2. What is the subject of the memo? _____

3. Who is the memo from? _____

4. Does the memo include a date, time, and place to meet? _____

5. Are there at least two blank spaces between the subject and the first

    paragraph? _____

☞ *Check your work on page 103. Record your score on page 108.*

ACTIVITY 6-3   YOUR GOAL: Get 4 or more answers correct.

Rewrite the following sentences using non-biased terms.

1. Mankind would be better off if our air was not polluted.

   _____

2. She applied for a position as a mailman.

   _____

3. The fireman worked 24-hour shifts.

   _____

4. Ask the stewardess for a blanket.

   _____

5. The foreman praised his employees.

   _____

☞ *Check your work on page 103. Record your score on page 108.*

UNIT 7

Business Letters

BUSINESS LETTERS

A business letter is the most frequently used form of written communication in the business world. It is a formal way to send a message outside of the office or business. A letter has certain advantages over a telephone conversation. The following are some of the advantages of writing a business letter:

- The sender has time to organize what must be said.
- The receiver has a copy of the message that he or she can refer to as a reminder.
- A written message often has more impact than conversation.

Parts of a Business Letter

In Unit 4, you learned the five parts of personal letters. Those parts were return address, letter address, salutation, body, and complimentary close. A business letter has seven parts. In addition to the five parts covered in Unit 4, the business letter has these following parts: keyed signature and title and reference initials.

The **keyed signature and title** includes the name of the person sending the letter and his or her job title. The keyed signature and title follows the complimentary close. Four spaces are allowed in between for the handwritten signature.

69

The **reference initials** are the initials of the person who keyed the letter. Two or three initials can be used. They are usually lowercase letters. Reference initials were covered in Unit 6.

Some optional parts of a letter are notations for enclosures and copies. An **enclosure notation** is added when something is being sent with the letter. A **copy notation** indicates that a copy of the letter was sent to the person or persons named.

Modified Block Style Format

The style or format of a letter refers to the placement of the date, paragraphs, and close. The two most widely used styles are the *block style* and *modified block style* formats. Unit 4 contains information and sample letters in block style. You may want to refresh your memory by reviewing Unit 4.

All lines in the **modified block style** format begin at the left margin except for the dateline, complimentary close, and keyed signature and title. These parts begin at the center point. Illustration 7-1 shows a modified block style letter.

Addresses and Salutations in Business Letters

Personal and business letters include a letter address and a salutation. The salutation matches the letter address. If the letter address is to a person, the salutation includes the name. For example, the salutation in a letter to Mr. David Valdez would be *Dear Mr. Valdez*. If the letter address is to a company, the salutation is *Ladies and Gentlemen*. The letter address always includes number and street name, city, two-letter state abbreviation, and ZIP Code. Many addresses use the ZIP Code plus four digits.

Closings in Business Letters

The most commonly used closings are *Very truly yours* and *Sincerely*. Other acceptable closings are *Sincerely yours* and *Yours very truly*. Capitalize the first letter of the first word.

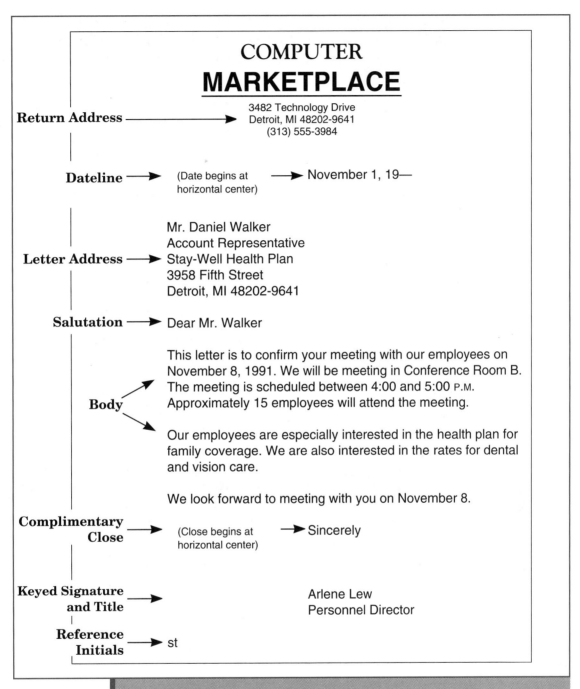

Illustration 7-1

Modified Block Style Letter

EVOLUTION OF WRITING—The Postal Service

The U.S. Postal Service is the largest single business in the world. The first Postal Act was added to the U.S. Constitution in 1789. The cost of mailing a letter was based on distance. One-page letters were charged as follows: not over 30 miles, 6 cents; not over 80 miles, 10 cents; not over 100 miles, 12.5 cents; greater distances, 25 cents. The first stamps were printed in 1847. The 10-cent Washington stamp and the 5-cent Franklin stamp were the first stamps issued. Today, the U.S. Postal Service moves over a half-billion pieces of mail every day. The use of high-speed electronic scanning equipment makes this possible.

 ## CHECKPOINT 7-1

YOUR GOAL:
Get 9 or more answers correct.

Rewrite each of the following addresses in correct business letter format in the space provided. Write the correct salutation after each address. The first one is completed as an example.

● Dr. Marilyn Chen, Valley Medical Center, 297 Speedway, Tucson, AZ 85711-8712. Use mixed punctuation.

Dr. Marilyn Chen

Valley Medical Center

297 Speedway

Tucson, AZ 85711-8712

Dear Dr. Chen:

1. Mr. Isiah Walton, General Manager, Las Posas Auto Parts, 4987 Las Posas Street, Chicago, IL 60605-7243. Use open punctuation.

2. Mrs. Nan Ott, Personnel Department, American Electronics Corporation, 765 Moana Blvd., Suite 34, Honolulu, HI 96813-7374. Use mixed punctuation.

1. _____   2. _____

   _____   _____

   _____   _____

   _____   _____

   _____   _____

☞ *Check your work on page 103. Record your score on page 109.*

TWO-LETTER STATE ABBREVIATIONS

The United States Postal Service has devised a two-letter state abbreviation for each state name. This abbreviation is used with a postal ZIP Code on all addresses. The two-letter state abbreviations are shown in Illustration 7-2. Study this listing so that you know each state's two-letter abbreviation.

Alabama ....AL	Idaho ....ID	Missouri ....MO	Pennsylvania............PA
Alaska ....AK	Illinois........................IL	Montana ....MT	Rhode Island ....RI
Arizona ....AZ	Indiana ....IN	Nebraska.............NE	South Carolina ....SC
Arkansas.................AR	Iowa ....IA	Nevada................NV	South Dakota ....SD
California.................CA	Kansas ....KS	New Hampshire ..NH	Tennesse ....TN
Colorado ....CO	Kentucky ....KY	New Jersey ....NJ	Texas ....TX
Connecticut ....CT	Louisiana ....LA	New Mexico........NM	Utah ....UT
Delaware.................DE	Maine.......................ME	New York ....NY	Vermont....................VT
District of	Maryland ....MD	North Carolina.....NC	Virginia ....VA
Columbia..............DC	Massachusetts ....MA	North Dakota.......ND	Washington ....WA
Florida.....................FL	Michigan ....MI	Ohio ....OH	West Virginia...........WV
Georgia...................GA	Minnesota...............MN	Oklahoma ....OK	Wisconsin ....WI
Hawaii ....HI	Mississippi ....MS	Oregon................OR	Wyoming ....WY

Illustration 7-2

Two-Letter State Abbreviations

CHECKPOINT 7-2

Write the two-letter state abbreviation in the space provided next to each of the following state names. The first one is complete as an example.

_____TX_____ ● Texas

_____ 1. Nebraska   _____ 2. West Virginia

_____ 3. Tennessee   _____ 4. South Dakota

_____ 5. New York   _____ 6. Oklahoma

_____ 7. Montana   _____ 8. Alaska

_____ 9. Iowa   _____ 10. Mississippi

☞ **Check your work on page 103. Record your score on page 109.**

GUIDELINES FOR WRITING LETTERS

These guidelines should be followed when writing a letter:

1. Plan your letters. Think about your purpose for writing before you begin.
2. Choose your words carefully. Be businesslike, but also be sincere and friendly. Use clear and concise language.
3. Be courteous. Show your readers that you respect them.
4. Be positive. Avoid negative words or accusations.
5. Be consistent in the format you use. If the date begins at the left margin, the closing should also begin at the left margin.
6. Letters should be keyed whenever possible. The dateline is keyed on line 16 for an average letter. Margins will be determined by the length of the letter.
7. Proofread letters for sentence structure, punctuation, capitalization, and spelling.

CLEAR AND CONCISE WRITING

Business letters are written to request something, to share information, or to follow-up on a request. Whatever the reason for writing, letters should be clear and concise. This will allow the reader to understand what the writer means and will avoid confusion.

The following are examples of the way to make letter writing clearer:

Example: Our copy machine is broken so we need to replace it. We are interested in buying one of your machines. Can your sales representative call us?

This is clearer:

Our office is interested in buying a new copy machine. We will be replacing our existing machine.

Please send us some information about your copy machines. We would also like a price list.

Please have your sales representative call us sometime next week.

Example: Sign and return the enclosed form as soon as possible.

This is clearer:

Please sign and return the enclosed form by January 15, 19—.

Example: You are invited to a retirement dinner for Martin Medina. It will be at the Oceanview Hotel on July 30. We hope you can attend.

This is clearer:

You are invited to a retirement dinner honoring Martin Medina. The dinner will be held at the Oceanview Hotel on July 30 at 6 P.M.

We know Martin will be pleased if you can attend this special evening. Please let us know by June 15 if you will be able to join us.

CHECKPOINT 7-3

YOUR GOAL:
Get 6 or more answers correct.

Write a letter to Ms. Anne Rossi, Sales Representative, Hi-Tech Business Machines, 3459 Grand Avenue, Detroit, Michigan 48202-2739.

The purpose of the letter is to tell Ms. Rossi of your company's plans to purchase a new computer. The computer is the XRT Model 348. You would like a price on the machine. You would also like to see a demonstration of the machine. Ask if the demonstration can be scheduled before May 15.

The letter is from Jim McBride, Purchasing Agent. Use modified block style and open punctuation. Use the current date. Key your letter if possible. Use blank paper. Assume that you have letterhead stationery in keying the dateline. Follow the guidelines for writing business letters.

Answer the following questions after keying or writing your letter. Write each answer in the space provided. The first one is completed as an example.

● What date did you use? _____ **Current date** _____

1. Where did you begin the date? _____

2. How many lines are in the letter address? _____

3. What is the salutation? _____

4. What computer did you write about? _____

5. How many spaces are before and after the salutation? _____

6. Where did you begin keying the closing? _____

7. What is the last part on the letter? _____

☞ **Check your work on page 103. Record your score on page 109.**

WHAT YOU HAVE LEARNED

As a result of completing this unit, you have learned to:

● There are seven parts in a business letter.
● The date and closing begin at the center point in a modified block style letter.
● Every state has a two-letter state abbreviation.
● Business letters must be written clearly and concisely.

ACTIVITY 7-1   **YOUR GOAL:** Get 4 or more answers correct.

Read the following letter. Answer the questions about the letter by writing *Yes* or *No* in the space provided. The first one is completed as an example.

Carla's Cabinet Construction

323 Broadway
Santa Monica, CA 90405-6838
(213) 555-9692

Sept 25, 19—

Mr. Arnold Rosenberg
Maintenance Supervisor
Heavy-Duty Maintenance Company
491 Industrial Parkway
Los Angeles, CA 90025-7463

Dear Mr. Rosenberg:
We are very dissatisfied with the equipment maintenance service we have received from your company. It is very important that your representative service our equipment once a month, as is stated in our agreement with your company.

There have been only four service calls made to us in the past six months. As a result, we have twice had to call you to have a table saw repaired.

We have had a service agreement with you for over 10 years. We would appreciate your immediate attention to this problem.

Very truly yours,

Carla Jones-Reyes
Owner

tf

_____**No**_____   ● Is the date written correctly?

_____   1. Does the letter use block style?

_____   2. Is the two-letter state abbreviation correct?

_____ 3. Is open punctuation used?

_____ 4. Should there be a double-space after the salutation?

_____ 5. Is the first paragraph written clearly?

_____ 6. Is there a double-space between each paragraph?

_____ 7. Should the closing begin at the left margin?

_____ 8. Is the closing capitalized correctly?

_____ 9. Are reference initials included?

_____ 10. Is the letter signed?

☞ **Check your work on page 104. Record your score on page 109.**

ACTIVITY 7-2   YOUR GOAL: Get 4 or more answers correct.

Write each letter in the space provided that correctly answers the following questions. The first one is completed as an example.

Which salutation uses mixed punctuation?

● __a__ a. Dear Dr. Oliver:

         b. Dear Ms. Hughes

         c. Dear Rev. Ogata

Which salutation uses mixed punctuation?

1. _____ a. Dear Dr. Oliver

          b. Dear Ms. Hughes:

          c. Dear Rev. Ogata

Which closing uses open punctuation?

2. _____ a. Sincerely yours,   3. _____ a. Very truly yours,

          b. Sincerely   b. Sincerely yours,

          c. Yours very truly,   c. Sincerely,

Which two-letter state abbreviation is correct?

4. _____ a. Las Vegas, NE   5. _____ a. Seattle, WN

          b. Austin, TX   b. Maui, HA

          c. Anchorage, AL   c. Denver, CO

☞ *Check your work on page 104. Record your score on page 109.*

3

PART

WRITING FOR PERSONAL DEVELOPMENT

UNIT 8   YOUR SELF-IMPROVEMENT ACTION PLAN

UNIT 8

Your Self-Improvement Action Plan

WHAT YOU WILL LEARN

When you finish this unit, you will be able to:

- Understand why setting goals in twelve categories is important.
- Set short-term and long-term goals.
- Develop a self-improvement action plan.

SETTING GOALS

Goals give meaning to life. A **goal** is something you want to achieve. Setting goals is one way to direct your future. Some goals are short term. **Short-term goals** can be achieved in a few days, a week, a month, or a year. Other goals are long term. **Long-term goals** take two to five years or longer to reach. Meeting goals depends on your outlook, age, and the steps you take.

This unit will help you set personal goals. Based on these goals, you will develop a self-improvement action plan. This action plan will be completed by answering four questions about where you are and where you want to be. The four questions are shown in Illustration 8-1.

CATEGORIES FOR SETTING GOALS

Your life can be divided into twelve different categories. Some categories may be more important to you than others. Writing down goals in each category will help focus on what you want. These goals will guide you in writing your self-improvement action plan. You want to live a balanced life. You need goals in all categories to live a balanced life. In each category there are questions to answer. Those categories and some possible questions are as follows:

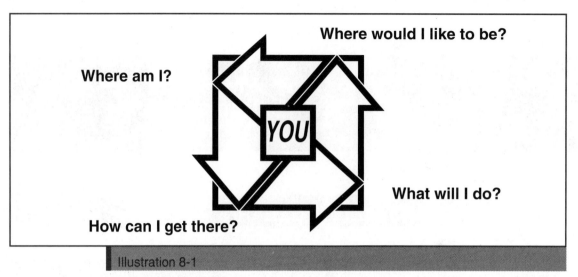

Illustration 8-1

Setting Goals—Four Questions to Answer

1. **Career.** If you are working, do you want a career change? If you are not working, what kind of job do you want? What will you look for in a job?
2. **Money.** How much money would you like to be earning? How much money do you spend? Would you like to save more?
3. **Education.** Would you like more job skills? Do you want to learn to play a musical instrument? Take a photography class or cooking class? Learn to use a computer?
4. **Social Relationships.** Would you like to have more friends? End some relationships? Improve some relationships?
5. **Family Relationships.** Would you like to improve communications with your spouse? Have a better understanding of your children? Be closer to relatives?
6. **Residence.** Would you like to move? Buy a house? Have another bedroom? Paint or redecorate?
7. **Transportation.** Would you like to buy a car? Would you like your present car to last longer?
8. **Travel.** Do you want to take a trip? Where would you go? For how long?
9. **Material Possessions.** What would you like to buy? A videocassette recorder? A new refrigerator? Is there something you would like to get rid of?
10. **Recreation.** What are your leisure-time activities? Do you make time for some fun in your life? Read a book once a month? Go to a movie or ball game?

11. **Physical Health.** Are you in good health? Would you like to exercise regularly? Lose five pounds? Get a physical checkup? Do you eat healthy foods?

12. **Wild Card.** This wild card category is a catch-all. What other areas do you want to work on? Do you have spiritual needs? Want to build your self-confidence?

This list will help you decide what you want from life. It will help you find out what is important to you. Answering these questions is the first step in writing your personal goals. There may be other questions you must answer for yourself. You need to be realistic when setting goals. Set goals that you can reach.

✔ CHECKPOINT 8-1

YOUR GOAL:
Complete 24 boxes.

Write down what you would like to be, do, or have in each category. Write one short-term goal and one long-term goal in each box. The Wild Card space is for you to create your own category. The first one is completed as an example.

Category	Short-Term Goals (Within one year)	Long-Term Goals (Two to five years)
● Career	*Complete high school computer accounting course.*	*Go to college to become an accountant.*
1. Career		
2. Money		

3. Education		
4. Social Relationships		
5. Family Relationships		
6. Residence		
7. Transportation		
8. Travel		
9. Material Possessions		

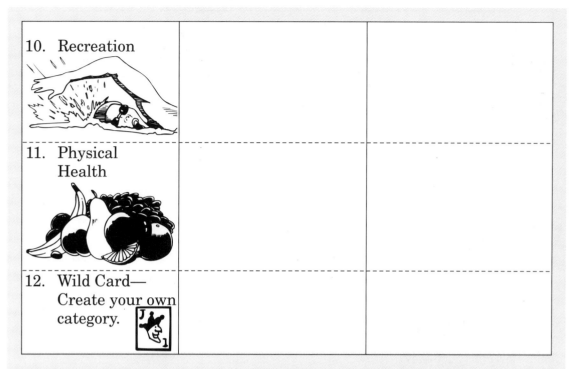

☞ **Check your work on page 104. Record your score on page 109.**

DEVELOPING YOUR ACTION PLAN

Goals are achieved by taking action. A plan for the action assures achievement within a set amount of time. To develop your action plan for your short- and long-term goals, you will need to answer these four questions:

1. *Where am I?* What you are now doing.
2. *Where would I like to be?* Your short- or long-term goal.
3. *How can I get there?* What you need to do.
4. *What will I do?* The actual action steps you will take to meet your goals. Be specific.

An example of how to answer these four questions is shown in Illustration 8-2. The category Money and a short-term goal are used.

Category	**Short-Term Goal**
Money	Develop a Monthly Budget

ACTION PLAN

1. Where am I?

   I do not budget or manage money wisely.

2. Where would I like to be?

   Become a better money manager.

3. How can I get there?

   Live within my monthly budget.

4. What will I do?

   a.) *Keep track of daily and weekly expenses.*

   b.) *Don't buy things I don't need.*

   c.) *Plan meals around sales items or use food coupons.*

Illustration 8-2

Self-Improvement Action Plan

WRITING GEMS—Don't Quit

When things go wrong as they sometimes will,
When the road you're trudging seems all uphill,
When the funds are low, and the debts are high,
And you want to smile, but you have to sigh,
When care is pressing you down a bit—
Rest if you must, but
don't you quit.

Success is failure turned inside out,
The silver tint of the clouds of doubt.
And you never can tell how close you are,
It may be near when it seems afar.
So, stick to the fight when you're hardest hit—
It's when things go wrong that
you mustn't quit.

Anonymous

CHECKPOINT 8-2

YOUR GOAL:
Get 4 or more answers.

Pick the category from Checkpoint 8-1 that is most important to you. Develop your action plan using the short-term goal you wrote for that category. Answer all four questions. Write in the space provided.

Category	Short-Term Goal
_____	_____
	_____
	_____

ACTION PLAN

1. Where am I?

_____

_____

_____

2. Where would I like to be?

_____

_____

3. How can I get there?

_____

_____

4. What will I do?

_____

_____

_____

_____

_____

_____

☞ **Check your work on page 104. Record your score on page 109.**

WHAT YOU HAVE LEARNED

As a result of completing this unit, you have learned:

● Setting short-term and long-term goals is one way to direct your future.

● Goals in all twelve categories are needed for living a balanced life.

● Four questions need to be answered to develop an action plan.

ACTIVITY 8-1   **YOUR GOAL:** Get 4 or more answers.

Pick another category from Checkpoint 8-1. Develop your action plan using the long-term goal you wrote in that category. Write in the spaces provided.

Category	Long-Term Goal
_____	_____
	_____
	_____

ACTION PLAN

1. Where am I?

_____

_____

_____

2. Where would I like to be?

_____

_____

3. How can I get there?

_____

_____

4. What will I do?

_____

_____

_____

_____

_____

_____

_____

☞ *Check your work on page 104. Record your score on page 109.*

CHECKING WHAT YOU LEARNED

Now you can see how much you have learned about writing for employment. These 50 questions cover the main topics you studied in this book. There is no time limit. When you finish, check your answers. Give yourself 1 point for each correct answer. Record your score on your Personal Progress Record. The evaluation chart will tell you where you may need additional study.

Put a check mark by each item that would be included in a Personal Profile.

1. _____ References
2. _____ Social Security Number
3. _____ Former Employers
4. _____ Schools Attended
5. _____ Salary History
6. _____ Names of Parents
7. _____ Telephone Number
8. _____ Honors and Awards

9. _____ Weight
10. _____ Special Skills
11. _____ Organizations
12. _____ Certificates Earned
13. _____ Work History
14. _____ Career Objective
15. _____ Hobbies

Match the information in the left column with one of the parts of a Personal Profile and Resume in the right column. Put the correct letter in each space provided.

16. _____ Mr. Frank Varges, Counselor
Silverado High School
375 Jordan Avenue
Indianapolis, IN 46204-1375
(317) 555-9327
17. _____ Career Objective: Police
Officer
18. _____ Speak German
19. _____ Good math and spelling skills
20. _____ Mark's Kitchen Cabinets
3475 Industrial Way
Albany, NY 12240-3475
Cabinet Maker — 4/86–3/91
21. _____ Voc-Tech Skills Center
2947 Hillcrest Road
Jackson, MS 39205-2947
(601) 555-4286 — 1990–Present
22. _____ Accounting Certificate

a. Career Objective

b. Educational Background

c. Work History

d. Skills and Abilities

e. Specialized Course and
Certificate

f. Interests, Talents, and
Aptitudes

g. References

Read the personal information on the following section of a job application. Put a check mark (✓) in the space provided next to the statements that are correct.

Previous employer	Dates (mo./yr.)		Current or last position	Salary (start/final)
Save Money Market	From 83	To 5/89	Salesperson	
Address			Telephone	
123 Pinal Ave., Scranton, PA 17109			(717) 555-6803	
Duties			Reason for leaving	
Waited on customers, stocked shelves, bagged groceries			Returned to School	

_____ 23. Dates include month and year.
_____ 24. Salary is included.
_____ 25. Job title is included.
_____ 26. Reason for leaving is completed.

Read each of the statements. If it is true write a **T** in the space provided. If it is false write an **F** in the space provided.

_____ 27. Reference initials are the writer's initials.
_____ 28. A return address is included in personal/business letters.
_____ 29. The salutation is the greeting in a letter.
_____ 30. Respectfully yours is a common complimentary close.
_____ 31. The letter address is placed before the salutation.
_____ 32. The message of the letter is the body.
_____ 33. Addresses in letters and envelopes do not need a ZIP code.
_____ 34. One of the basic rules when completing forms is to write neatly or key the information.
_____ 35. An Equal Opportunity Information Form includes questions about your ethnic background.
_____ 36. Form W-4 is required by the Internal Revenue Service.
_____ 37. Form W-4 tells your employer how many children you have.
_____ 38. Form I-9, Employment Eligibility Verification, is required by the Department of the Treasury.
_____ 39. A sales slip is one of the most common business forms.
_____ 40. A memo is a written communication used within an office or a business.
_____ 41. A memo has a heading that only includes the DATE and SUBJECT.
_____ 42. Reference initials are the first letters of the first and last names of the person who keyed the correspondence.
_____ 43. Block style is one of the most widely used letter styles.

_____ 44. State abbreviations are used with postal ZIP Codes on all addresses.

_____ 45. The two-letter state abbreviation for Arizona is AR.

_____ 46. You should proofread letters for punctuation and capitalization.

_____ 47. A short-term goal can be achieved in a few days, a week, a month, or a year.

_____ 48. In setting goals one of the questions to ask yourself is, "Where am I?"

_____ 49. A self-improvement plan should include short- and long-term goals.

_____ 50. One of the categories to think about in developing goals is your education goals.

☞ *Check your work on page 104. Record your score on page 109.*

GLOSSARY

A

Allowance A person who is dependent on you for support.

B

Block Style A letter format in which all parts begin at the left margin.
Body The message in a letter.

C

Complimentary Close The ending in a letter.
Copy Notation Indicates that a copy of the letter was sent to the person or persons named.

D

Dependents People other than your wife or husband that you support. Children and elderly parents may be dependents.

E

Enclosure Notation Indicates that something is being sent with the letter.
Equal Opportunity Hiring practice in which an employer will hire a person regardless of gender, sexual preference, race, creed, color, religion, handicap, or veteran's status.
Exempt Status A claim that allows you to have no federal income tax withheld from your paycheck. You may claim to be exempt if you will not earn enough to owe any federal tax.

F

Form I-9, Employment Eligibility Verification A standard form used to verify that an individual is eligible to work in the United States.

Form W-4, Employee's Withholding Allowance Certificate A form completed for income tax withholding purposes.

G

Goal Something you want to achieve.

H

Head of Household An unmarried person who pays more than 50 percent of household expenses.

K

Keyed Signature and Title The typed name of the person sending the letter and his or her job title.

L

Letter Address The name and address of the person receiving the letter.
Long-term Goal A goal that can be achieved in two to five years or longer.

M

Memo A written communication used within an office or business.
Mixed Punctuation A colon is used after the salutation, but a comma appears after the complimentary close.
Modified Block Style A letter format in which all lines in a letter begin at the left margin except for the date and complimentary close.

O

Open Punctuation No punctuation appears after the salutation or complimentary close.

P

Penalty of Perjury A person may be fined or go to prison for giving false information.

R

Reference Initials The first letters of the first and last names of the person who keyed the correspondence, if it was not the sender.

Resume A summary of a person's background and qualifications.

Return Address The writer's address.

S

Salutation A greeting to the person receiving the letter.

Short-term Goal A goal that can be achieved in a few days, a week, a month, or a year.

Signature The letter writer's name written in longhand.

Spouse A wife or husband.

INDEX

ANSWERS

✓ CHECKING WHAT YOU KNOW

1. ✓	26. ✓
2. ✓	27. f
3. ✓	28. g
4. ✓	29. d
5. ✓	30. e
6.	31. c
7. ✓	32. b
8. ✓	33. a
9.	34. T
10. ✓	35. T
11. ✓	36. F
12. ✓	37. T
13. ✓	38. T
14. ✓	39. T
15. ✓	40. F
16. g	41. T
17. d	42. T
18. e	43. F
19. a	44. F
20. c	45. T
21. f	46. T
22. b	47. T
23.	48. T
24. ✓	49. F
25.	50. T

UNIT 1

CHECKPOINT 1-1, page 4

Personal Information
Give yourself 1 point for each item.
1. Name
2. Address
3. Telephone number
4. Social Security number
5. Date of birth
6. Driver's license number

CHECKPOINT 1-2, page 5

Educational Background
Give yourself 1 point for each item.
1. Name of school
2. Address
3. Dates attended

CHECKPOINT 1-3, page 6

Specialized Courses and Certificates
Give yourself 1 point for each item.
1. Name of school
2. Name of specialized course or certificate
3. Date(s)

CHECKPOINT 1-4, page 7

Extracurricular Activities and Organizations
Give yourself 1 point for each item.
List of extracurricular activities
Name of organization(s) or group(s)

CHECKPOINT 1-5, page 7

Honors and Awards
Give yourself 1 point for each item.
Name of honor(s) or award(s)

CHECKPOINT 1-6, page 8

Work History
Give yourself 1 point for each item.
Each paid job should have
1. Name of employer
2. Address
3. Job title or job duties
4. Dates employed
5. Supervisor and telephone number
6. Starting and final salary
7. Reason for leaving

CHECKPOINT 1-7, page 9

Skills and Abilities
Give yourself 1 point for each item.
List of each special skill and ability

CHECKPOINT 1-8, page 9

Interests, Talents, and Aptitudes
Give yourself 1 point for each item.
List of interests, talents, and aptitudes

CHECKPOINT 1-9, page 10

Career Objective
Give yourself 1 point for each item.
1. Name(s) of jobs qualified for
2. Career goal

CHECKPOINT 1-10, page 11

References
Give yourself 1 point for each item.
Each reference should have
1. Name and title
2. Address
3. Telephone number

ACTIVITY 1-1, page 13

1. g	5. b
2. d	6. f
3. e	7. c
4. a	

UNIT 2

CHECKPOINT 2-1, page 14

1. False	4. False
2. True	5. False
3. True	

CHECKPOINT 2-2, page 18

1. Your name
2. Street or P.O. box
3. City, state, ZIP Code
4. Area code and telephone number

CHECKPOINT 2-3, page 19

1. Your Career Objective

CHECKPOINT 2-4, page 19

Give yourself 10 points. Subtract 1 point for each misspelled word and each date left out.

CHECKPOINT 2-5, page 19

Give yourself 10 points. Subtract 1 point for each misspelled word and each date left out.

CHECKPOINT 2-6, page 19

Give yourself 1 point for each special skill.

CHECKPOINT 2-7, page 20

Give yourself 10 points. Subtract 1 point for each misspelled word and each incomplete name and address.

CHECKPOINT 2-8, page 21

1. 1987-89-Automotive Technical Institute
   Detroit, Michigan
   Received Automotive
   Mechanic Certificate
2. 1986-87-Yee's Foreign Car Repair
   Auto Mechanic Assistant

ACTIVITY 2-1, page 22

1. Personal Information
2. Objective
3. Education
4. Experience
5. Skills and Abilities
6. References

ACTIVITY 2-2, page 22

1. <u>V</u>ocational
   <u>O</u>klahoma
   <u>C</u>onstruction P<u>r</u>ogram
2. Mana<u>g</u>er
   <u>E</u>mporium
   Stre<u>et</u>
   <u>OR</u>
   No area code
3. <u>M</u>r. <u>O</u>saki
   <u>A</u>pprenticeship
   <u>S</u>uite
   <u>E</u>ugene
   Incomplete phone number

UNIT 3

CHECKPOINT 3-1, page 26

1. Did you print plainly? Yes ___ No ___
2. Did you write your
   last name first? Yes ___ No ___
3. Did you include your
   ZIP Code? Yes ___ No ___
4. Did you include the
   area code with your
   telephone number? Yes ___ No ___
5. Is your Social Security
   number accurate? Yes ___ No ___

Give yourself 1 point for each Yes answer.

CHECKPOINT 3-2, page 27

1. Did you answer three
   items on the first line? Yes ___ No ___
2. Did you answer either
   Section B or Sections
   A and B?   Yes ___ No ___

Give yourself 1 point for each Yes answer.

CHECKPOINT 3-3, page 28

1. Did you print plainly? Yes ___ No ___
2. Do the addresses
   include street, city,
   state, and ZIP Code?   Yes ___ No ___

Give yourself 1 point for each Yes answer.

CHECKPOINT 3-4, page 30

1. Is your current job
   listed first? If not
   working, is your last
   job listed first?   Yes ___ No ___
2. For each job listed,
   was the following
   completed?
   a. Dates employed
      include month and
      year   Yes ___ No ___
   b. Current or last
      position   Yes ___ No ___
   c. Starting and final
      salary   Yes ___ No ___
   d. Address including
      city, state, and ZIP
      Code   Yes ___ No ___
   e. Telephone number Yes ___ No ___
   f. Duties   Yes ___ No ___
   g. Reason for leaving Yes ___ No ___

Give yourself 1 point for each Yes answer.

CHECKPOINT 3-5, page 31

1. Did you include at
   least two references? Yes ___ No ___
2. Does each reference
   address include city,
   state, and ZIP Code?   Yes ___ No ___
3. Is the telephone number
   included for each
   reference?   Yes ___ No ___

Give yourself 1 point for each Yes answer.

CHECKPOINT 3-6, page 32

1. Did you sign the
   application?   Yes ___ No ___
2. Did you date the
   application?   Yes ___ No ___

Give yourself 1 point for each Yes answer.

ACTIVITY 3-1, page 34

1. a	2. b	3. a	4. a
c	d	c	b
		d	c

Give yourself 1 point for each correct
answer.

UNIT 4

CHECKPOINT 4-1, page 38

1. a	2. f
3. g	4. b
5. h	6. d
7. c	

CHECKPOINT 4-2, page 40

1. Does your letter include these parts?
   Return address and
   date   Yes ___ No ___
   Letter address   Yes ___ No ___
   Salutation   Yes ___ No ___
   Closing   Yes ___ No ___
2. Did you use open
   punctuation?   Yes ___ No ___
3. Did you state the
   position you are
   applying for?   Yes ___ No ___
4. Did you ask for an
   interview?   Yes ___ No ___
5. Does your letter look
   neat and attractive?   Yes ___ No ___
6. Did you sign the
   letter?   Yes ___ No ___

Give yourself 1 point for each Yes answer.
Get an extra point if all words are spelled
correctly.

CHECKPOINT 4-3, page 41

1. True	2. True
3. False	4. True
5. True	

CHECKPOINT 4-4, page 43

1. Does your letter include these parts?
   Return address and
   date   Yes ___ No ___
   Letter address   Yes ___ No ___
   Salutation   Yes ___ No ___
   Closing   Yes ___ No ___
2. Did you use mixed
   punctuation?   Yes ___ No ___
3. Did you say thank you
   in the opening
   paragraph?   Yes ___ No ___
4. Did you reaffirm
   your interest and
   availability?   Yes ___ No ___
5. Does your letter look
   neat and attractive? Yes ___ No ___
6. Did you sign the
   letter?   Yes ___ No ___

Give yourself 1 point for each Yes answer.
Get an extra point if all words are spelled
correctly.

CHECKPOINT 4-5, page 44

1. Does both the return address and
   receiver's address include these parts?
   Two-letter state
   abbreviation   Yes ___ No ___
   ZIP Code   Yes ___ No ___
2. Are addresses in all
   capital letters with
   no punctuation? Yes ___ No ___
3. Is the letter folded
   correctly?   Yes ___ No ___

Give yourself 1 point for each Yes answer.

ACTIVITY 4-1, page 45

1. Does your letter include these parts?
   Return address and
   date   Yes ___ No ___
   Letter address   Yes ___ No ___
   Salutation   Yes ___ No ___
   Closing   Yes ___ No ___

2. Did you use open
   punctuation?   Yes ___ No ___
3. Did you state the
   position you are
   applying for?   Yes ___ No ___
4. Did you ask for an
   interview?   Yes ___ No ___
5. Does your letter look
   neat and attractive? Yes ___ No ___
6. Did you sign the
   letter?   Yes ___ No ___

Give yourself 1 point for each Yes answer.
Get an extra point if all words are spelled
correctly.

ACTIVITY 4-2, page 45

1. Does both the return address and
   receiver's address include these parts?
   Two-letter state
   abbreviation   Yes ___ No ___
   ZIP Code   Yes ___ No ___
2. Are addresses in all
   capital letters with
   no punctuation? Yes ___ No ___
3. Is the letter folded
   correctly?   Yes ___ No ___

Give yourself 1 point for each Yes answer.

UNIT 5

CHECKPOINT 5-1, page 50

Each section should have one item
marked. Give yourself 4 points.

CHECKPOINT 5-2, page 51

1. Does Line G equal the
   total of Lines A
   through F?   Yes ___ No ___
2. Is the first name
   written first?   Yes ___ No ___

3. Is the home address
   included?   Yes ___ No ___
4. Are the city and state
   included?   Yes ___ No ___
5. Is the ZIP Code
   included?   Yes ___ No ___
6. Are there nine digits
   in the Social Security
   number?   Yes ___ No ___
7. Is one box marked for
   marital status?   Yes ___ No ___
8. Is Line 4 the same
   number written in
   Line G?   Yes ___ No ___
9. Is Line 7 marked?   Yes ___ No ___
10. Is the form signed?   Yes ___ No ___
11. Is the form dated?   Yes ___ No ___
12. Is information printed
    except for signature?   Yes ___ No ___

Give yourself 1 point for each Yes answer.

CHECKPOINT 5-3, page 54

1. Is the last name
   written first?   Yes ___ No ___
2. Is the birth name
   included?   Yes ___ No ___
3. Is the address
   included?   Yes ___ No ___
4. Are the city and state
   included?   Yes ___ No ___
5. Is the ZIP Code
   included?   Yes ___ No ___
6. Is the date of birth
   included?   Yes ___ No ___
7. Are boxes 1, 2, or 3
   marked?   Yes ___ No ___
8. Is the form signed?   Yes ___ No ___
9. Is the form dated?   Yes ___ No ___
10. Is the information
    printed except for the
    signature?   Yes ___ No ___

Give yourself 1 point for each Yes answer.

CHECKPOINT 5-4, page 57

Give yourself 10 points. Subtract 1 point for each error.

SPORTS UNLIMITED
458 PARK ST.
BOSTON, MA 02107-1234
(617) 555-3846

DATE *Current Date*

SOLD TO *Barry Cowan*
ADDRESS *1248 Oak St., Denver, CO 80232-*
SHIP TO   *1248*
ADDRESS

QUANTITY	DESCRIPTION	PRICE	AMOUNT
1	*J. V. Sports Shoes*		29 95
		TAX	1 80
		TOTAL	31 75

CASH   CHARGE ✓   SOLD BY *KYT*

ACTIVITY 5-1, page 58

1. Dameron
2. 546-27-6831
3. Single
4. Tampa, Florida
5. 1

ACTIVITY 5-2, page 59

1. December 15, 19—
2. Rachel Acosta
3. Cash
4. four; remember the two pairs of socks
5. $1.80

UNIT 6

CHECKPOINT 6-1, page 62

1. Arnold Stein
2. Parking Lot C Resurfacing
3. March 8
4. Parking Lots A or B, street parking
5. ef

CHECKPOINT 6-2, page 62

1. Ms. Lilly Dong
2. Vacation
3. No
4. Your name
5. Yes

CHECKPOINT 6-3, page 64

1. mail carrier
2. fire fighter
3. enclosed
4. work force
5. thank you
6. we think
7. because
8. humanity
9. flight attendant
10. supervisor

ACTIVITY 6-1, page 66

1. No   2. Yes
3. No   4. No
5. Yes

ACTIVITY 6-2, page 66

1. Co-workers, employees, or names of specific people
2. Car pool
3. Your name
4. Yes
5. Yes

ACTIVITY 6-3, page 68

1. **Everyone** would be better off if our air was not polluted.
2. She applied for a position as a **mail carrier.**

3. The **fire fighter** worked 24-hour shifts.
4. Ask the **flight attendant** for a blanket.
5. The **supervisor** praised his employees.

UNIT 7

CHECKPOINT 7-1, page 72

Give yourself 1 point for each correct answer.

1. Mr. Isiah Walton, General Manager
   Las Posas Auto Parts
   4987 Las Posas Street
   Chicago, IL 60605-7243

   Dear Mr. Walton

2. Mrs. Nan Ott
   Personnel Department
   American Electronics Corporation
   765 Moana Blvd., Suite 34
   Honolulu, HI 96813-7374

   Dear Mrs. Ott:

CHECKPOINT 7-2, page 74

1. NE   2. WV
3. TN   4. SD
5. NY   6. OK
7. MT   8. AK
9. IA   10. MS

CHECKPOINT 7-3, page 76

1. Horizontal center, after letterhead
2. four or five (Ms. Anne Rossi, Sales Representative can be on one or two lines)
3. Dear Ms. Rossi
4. XRT Model 348
5. one blank or double-space
6. Horizontal center, double-space below body
7. Reference initials

ACTIVITY 7-1, page 77
1. No
2. Yes
3. No
4. Yes
5. Yes
6. Yes
7. No
8. No
9. Yes
10. No

ACTIVITY 7-2, page 78
1. b
2. b
3. a
4. b
5. c

UNIT 8

CHECKPOINT 8-1, page 85

A short-term and long-term goal is written in at least 10 categories. Give yourself 1 point for each box completed.

CHECKPOINT 8-2, page 89

The goal category and short-term goal are filled in. All four questions are answered. Specific things you will do are listed in Question 4. Give yourself 1 point for each answer to Questions 1-4. Give yourself 1 point for the category and short-term goal.

ACTIVITY 8-1, page 90

All four questions are answered. Specific things you will do are listed in Question 4. Give yourself 1 point for writing the category and long-term goal. Give yourself 1 point for each answer to the four questions.

✔ CHECKING WHAT YOU LEARNED

1. ✓		26. ✓
2. ✓		27. F
3. ✓		28. T
4. ✓		29. T
5. ✓		30. F
6.		31. T
7. ✓		32. T
8. ✓		33. F
9.		34. T
10. ✓		35. T
11. ✓		36. T
12. ✓		37. F
13. ✓		38. F
14. ✓		39. T
15. ✓		40. T
16. g		41. F
17. a		42. T
18. d		43. T
19. f		44. T
20. c		45. F
21. b		46. T
22. e		47. T
23.		48. T
24.		49. T
25. ✓		50. T

PERSONAL PROGRESS RECORD

Name _____

Use the chart below to determine the areas in which you need to do the most work. In the space provided, write the total number of points you earned for each content area. Add up the total number of points you earned to find your final score. Circle those items you answered correctly. As you begin your study, pay close attention to those areas that you missed.

Content Area	Item Number	Study Pages	Total Points	Number Right
UNIT 1 — A Personal Profile				
and				
UNIT 2 — Resume				
Personal Information	2, 6, 7, 9	4, 16–17	4	☐
Educational Background	4, 8, 11, 12, 18, 22	4, 16–17	6	☐
Work History	1, 3, 5, 13, 20	7, 16–17	5	☐
Skills and Abilities	10, 17	8, 16–17	2	☐
Interests, Talents, and Aptitudes	15, 21	9	2	☐
Career Objective	14, 19	9, 16–17	2	☐
References	16	11, 16–17	1	☐
UNIT 3 — Job Applications				
Personal Information	23, 24, 25, 26	25	4	☐

Content Area	Item Number	Study Pages	Total Points	Number Right
UNIT 5 — Forms				
Basic Rules	34	49	1	☐
Equal Opportunity Form	35	49	1	☐
Form W-4	36, 37	50	2	☐
Form I-9	38	53	1	
Sales Slips	39	55, 56	1	☐
UNIT 6 — Memos				
Business Memos	40, 41	60	2	☐
UNIT 4 — Personal/Business Letters				
and				
UNIT 7 — Business Letters				
Guidelines/ Styles	43, 46	36, 37	2	☐
Parts of Letter Return Address	31	38, 39	1	☐
Letter Address	30	38, 39, 70	1	☐
Salutation	27	38, 39, 70	1	☐
Body	33	38, 39	1	☐
Complimentary Close	28	38, 39, 70	1	☐
Signature	32, 42	38, 39, 69	2	☐
Reference Initials	29	60, 70	1	☐
ZIP Codes	44	73	1	☐
Two-Letter Abbreviations	45	73	1	☐

Content Area	Item Number	Study Pages	Total Points	Number Right

UNIT 8 — Your Self-Improvement Action Plan

Setting Goals	47, 48, 49	83	3	
Goal Categories	50	83, 84	1	

Date _____   Total Points: 50   Your Score: [____]

UNIT 1: A Personal Profile

Exercise	Score
Checkpoint 1-1	_____
Checkpoint 1-2	_____
Checkpoint 1-3	_____
Checkpoint 1-4	_____
Checkpoint 1-5	_____
Checkpoint 1-6	_____
Checkpoint 1-7	_____
Checkpoint 1-8	_____
Checkpoint 1-9	_____
Checkpoint 1-10	_____
Activity 1-1	_____
Total	_____

HOW ARE YOU DOING?

25 or better	Excellent
24	Good
23	Fair
Less than 23	See Instructor

UNIT 2: Resume

Exercise	Score
Checkpoint 2-1	_____
Checkpoint 2-2	_____
Checkpoint 2-3	_____
Checkpoint 2-4	_____
Checkpoint 2-5	_____
Checkpoint 2-6	_____
Checkpoint 2-7	_____
Checkpoint 2-8	_____
Activity 2-1	_____
Activity 2-2	_____
Total	_____

HOW ARE YOU DOING?

60 or better	Excellent
55–59	Good
50–54	Fair
Less than 50	See Instructor

UNIT 3: Job Applications

Exercise	Score
Checkpoint 3-1	_____
Checkpoint 3-2	_____
Checkpoint 3-3	_____
Checkpoint 3-4	_____
Checkpoint 3-5	_____
Checkpoint 3-6	_____
Activity 3-1	_____
Total	_____

HOW ARE YOU DOING?

27 or better	Excellent
26	Good
25	Fair
Less than 25	See Instructor

UNIT 4: Personal/Business Letters

Exercise	Score
Checkpoint 4-1	_____
Checkpoint 4-2	_____
Checkpoint 4-3	_____
Checkpoint 4-4	_____
Checkpoint 4-5	_____
Activity 4-1	_____
Activity 4-2	_____
Total	_____

HOW ARE YOU DOING?

36 or better	Excellent
35	Good
34	Fair
Less than 34	See Instructor

UNIT 5: Forms

Exercise	Score
Checkpoint 5-1	_____
Checkpoint 5-2	_____
Checkpoint 5-3	_____
Checkpoint 5-4	_____
Activity 5-1	_____
Activity 5-2	_____
Total	_____

HOW ARE YOU DOING?

40 or better	Excellent
36–39	Good
32–35	Fair
Less than 32	See Instructor

UNIT 6: Memos

Exercise	Score
Checkpoint 6-1	_____
Checkpoint 6-2	_____
Checkpoint 6-3	_____
Activity 6-1	_____
Activity 6-2	_____
Activity 6-3	_____
Total	_____

HOW ARE YOU DOING?

29 or better	Excellent
27–28	Good
25–26	Fair
Less than 25	See Instructor

UNIT 7: Business Letters

Exercise	Score
Checkpoint 7-1	_____
Checkpoint 7-2	_____
Checkpoint 7-3	_____
Activity 7-1	_____
Activity 7-2	_____
Total	_____

HOW ARE YOU DOING?

37 or better	Excellent
35–36	Good
33–34	Fair
Less than 33	See Instructor

UNIT 8: Your Self-Improvement Action Plan

Exercise	Score
Checkpoint 8-1	_____
Checkpoint 8-2	_____
Activity 8-1	_____
Total	_____

HOW ARE YOU DOING?

28 or better	Excellent
26–27	Good
24–25	Fair
Less than 24	See Instructor

✔ CHECKING WHAT YOU LEARNED

Use the chart below to determine the areas in which you need to do the most review. In the space provided, write the total number of points you earned for each content area. Add up the total number of points you earned to find your final score. Circle those items you answered correctly. Review those areas that you missed.

Content Area	Item Number	Study Pages	Total Points	Number Right

UNIT 1 — A Personal Profile

and

UNIT 2 — Resume

Content Area	Item Number	Study Pages	Total Points	Number Right
Personal Information	2, 6, 7, 9	4, 16, 17	4	☐
Educational Background	4, 8, 11, 12, 21, 22	4, 16, 17	6	☐
Work History	3, 5, 13, 20	7, 16, 17	4	☐
Skills and Abilities	10, 18	8, 16, 17	2	☐

Content Area	Item Number	Study Pages	Total Points	Number Right
Interests, Talents, and Aptitudes	15, 19	9	2	
Career Objective	14, 17	9, 16, 17	2	
References	1, 16	11, 16, 17	2	

UNIT 3 — Job Applications

Content Area	Item Number	Study Pages	Total Points	Number Right
Work History	23, 24, 25, 26	29	4	

UNIT 5 — Forms

Content Area	Item Number	Study Pages	Total Points	Number Right
Basic Rules	34	49	1	
Equal Opportunity Form	35	49	1	
Form W-4	36, 37	50	2	
Form I-9	38	53	1	
Sales Slips	39	55, 56	1	

UNIT 6 — Memos

Content Area	Item Number	Study Pages	Total Points	Number Right
Business Memos	40, 41	60	2	

UNIT 4 — Personal/Business Letters

and

UNIT 7 — Business Letters

Content Area	Item Number	Study Pages	Total Points	Number Right
Guidelines/ Styles	43, 46	36, 37	2	
Parts of Letter Return Address	28	38, 39	1	
Letter Address	31	38, 39, 70	1	
Salutation	29	38, 39, 70	1	
Body	32	38, 39	1	

Content Area	Item Number	Study Pages	Total Points	Number Right
Complimentary Close	30	38, 39, 70	1	
Signature	32	38, 39, 60	1	
Reference Initials	27, 42	60, 70	2	
ZIP Codes	33	70	1	
Two-Letter Abbreviations	44, 45	73	1	

UNIT 8 — Your Self-Improvement Action Plan

Content Area	Item Number	Study Pages	Total Points	Number Right
Setting Goals	47, 48, 49	83	3	
Goal Categories	50	83, 84	1	

Date _____   Total Points: 50   Your Score: [   ]